ANTICIPATING REVIVAL

K. BOBIE AMANKWATIA,
DMIN

ANTICIPATING REVIVAL

POSITIONING THE CHURCH FOR FRESH FIRE

INLIC - BOBIE BOOKS

TABLE OF CONTENTS

COPYRIGHT

Other works by the author:

- Phases of Revival
- Revival Leadership vol. 1
- Restoring True Worship
- Anointed Leadership

DEDICATION

To my beloved mother, Dora, a centenarian and an anointed woman of God, whose life has been a testament of unwavering faith, integrity, and boundless compassion. You have nurtured and guided your sons with wisdom and grace and have also been a mother to many, offering encouragement and love to all who crossed your path. Your legacy of strength, humility, and godly counsel continues to inspire us all. This book is dedicated to you, a true vessel of God's love and a pillar of virtue.

ACKNOWLEDGMENTS

Above all, I lift my heart in profound and boundless gratitude to the Lord Almighty for His immeasurable grace in blessing my beloved mother, Dora, with a century of life. Reaching her 100th birthday is a testimony to the Lord's divine favor, His sustaining hand, and the richness of His mercy. To God alone be all the Glory!

To the greatest gift God has given me subsequent to my salvation, my darling wife, Tonya, I owe a debt of love and appreciation that words can scarcely capture. Your unwavering support, encouragement, and tireless inspiration have driven the completion of this volume. You are my anchor, my joy, and my steadfast companion in this journey.

I also extend my deepest and heartfelt thanks to the terrific trio, Scott Bobie Amankwatia, Daniel Opoku Amankwatia, and Asamoah Gyawu Amankwatia (Jr), for their unwavering loyalty and their moving reflections on the life and legacy of their grand-mother. Your support has been a gift, and your beautiful tributes breathe life into this dedication.

INTRODUCTION

In a world gripped by unprecedented social unrest, moral decadence, and rapid spiritual deterioration, many find themselves overwhelmed by the gloom and doom that seems to creep ever closer. The foreboding uncertainty of our civilization's future haunts countless souls, pondering the consequences of cultural decay and a godless society in a relentless push to exclude God from society. It is as if the floodgates have opened, and everyone is doing what seems right in their eyes, mirroring the unsettling times depicted in Judges 21:25.

The chaos rapidly spreading like wildfire and the governments' apparent incompetence all contribute to the population's feelings of hopelessness, anxiety, and despair. Even those who profess faith in Christ are left wondering if we are approaching the end of the world. Once a beacon of hope, the Church is often viewed as an impotent bystander, losing its relevance in a rapidly changing culture.

Anticipating Revival: ***Positioning The Church For Fresh Fire*** offers hope amidst societal turmoil. The book artfully blends scriptural wisdom and historical insights, guiding readers through challenging times of spiritual and moral uncertainties and turning them into platforms for spiritual revival.

Drawing on decades of ministering in diverse and often challenging environments, the author shares breakthroughs from the Lord, revealing instances of His revival among His people in response to the Church's earnest prayers. This perspective solidifies the conviction that difficult times do not imply that we surrender but instead bend our knees in prayer, seeking the Lord's intervention.

Exploring the term "revival," laden with diverse emotions, we delve into it as a mighty spiritual force that elicits hope, restoration, and transformation. Throughout history, we've witnessed this phenomenon in revivals such as the Wesleyan, Businessman Prayer, Azusa Street, Pyongyang (Jerusalem of the East), and the Lewis Islands Revivals, where it catalyzed societal change.

Instead of succumbing to anger and finger-pointing, which have become so common in some pulpits today, the Church, drawing inspiration from past historical revivals, actively pursues an outpouring of Fresh Fire to renew and impact the culture.

Specifically, **Anticipating Revival** delves into the essence and significance of revival for the Church, acknowledging that moments of crisis or spiritual drought often precede revival. It highlights the Church's role as a spiritual flashlight in exposing and dispelling the darkness.

The book explores preparation for the Holy Spirit's visitation, aiming to awaken dormant churches and struggling communities. The seven-fold purposes for revival, including soul salvation, backslider restoration, believer unity, and societal renewal, underscore that revival is not only for personal renewal and transformation but also for influencing communities and nations through the Holy Spirit's power.

However, pursuing revival demands more than anticipation. The Church must confront threats and satanic harassment with a willingness to die to self and embrace the Cross. Prayer becomes the key to igniting revival, necessitating a shift in mindset, practices, and priorities toward godly pursuits.

It is crucial to recognize that a spiritual revival is not a singular event but an ongoing journey requiring vigilance against forces or factors that may quench its fire. Identifying and interrupting elements that hinder revival and the strategies to avoid them is a focal point in this book.

As readers embark on this remarkable journey to anticipate revival and position themselves for Fresh Fire, the ultimate aim is to transform the world by demonstrating the power of the Gospel of Jesus Christ (see Acts 8:4-8).

Anticipating Revival calls believers to rise above challenges, embrace prayer, and become vessels for the Holy Spirit's renewal—a summons to reclaim the relevance of the Church in a world desperately in need of healing and restoration.

RUDE AWAKENING BEFORE A GREAT AWAKENING

O Lord, I have heard Your speech and was afraid; O Lord, revive Your work in the midst of the years! In the midst of the years, make it known; In wrath, remember mercy – Habakkuk 3:2.

We are on the verge of a rude awakening in a tumultuous new era of gloom and doom. An era full of uncertainties, anguish, and despair. There has never been such an unleashing of satanic influence in the modern world as there is today. It is like Satan is ferociously and vengefully spewing from the pit of hell its filth in lawlessness, violence, murder, rape, drug and alcohol abuse, over-sexualization of the culture, and suicide, especially the youth.

Like Prophet Habakkuk, those sensitive to His promptings of the Spirit are crying out, "O Lord, I have heard Your speech and was afraid; O Lord, revive Your work in the midst of the years! Amid the years, make it known; In wrath remember mercy" (Habakkuk 3:2). The Lord stands by His covenant people even in challenging times.

The Church is the only agency on earth that can deal with evil in both the spiritual and the physical realm to bring healing and restoration to our communities. Therefore, we cannot lose heart; instead, we must bend our knees before the Lord for a release of an outpouring of the Spirit to awaken His people and torch the nations with revival fire.

A new outbreak of revival can bring about the necessary social and political changes to save humanity from self-inhalation, just as the Wesleyan Revivals kept Britain from going into revolutionary wars like their French neighbors. A release of Fresh Fire is needed more desperately today than ever.

The saints of old saw their day's dark times of spiritual and moral deterioration as platforms of opportunity to seek the Lord for spiritual awakening. Their attitude towards the decadence of their day was not to react, make excuses, nor resort to finger-pointing at society but instead to respond with repentant hearts and a renewed vigor for prayer and intercession for revival. They did not sit still in self-pity and complain.

But why should they? The Church is the world's lighthouse, reflecting the indwelling God – the "... Light in Him there is no darkness at all" (1 John 1:15). Therefore, the Church cannot cut and run, but shine like a flashlight to dispel the darkness. A little spark of light can overpower mountains of thick darkness. The Lord has positioned the Church to do just that in these dark times of doom and gloom as the salt and light (see Matthew 5:13-16). The Church is the only hope for our rapidly deteriorating society.

Many devout men and women of the faith have sounded the alarm throughout the history of the Church. Let us reflect on what past Christian leaders and Revivalists had to say about what the role of the Church should be in dark times:

John Wesley - "The world is in darkness, and only a great spiritual awakening can bring it back to the light. Let us pray for revival, that the light of Christ may shine brightly in our hearts and the world around us."

Billy Graham - "When a nation is in moral decay, God's people must cry out to Him for revival. When the church is weak, it must plead for a fresh outpouring of the Holy Spirit. Revival is God's answer to a nation and a church that has turned their backs on Him."

Jonathan Edwards - "In times of moral decay and spiritual decline, the only hope for a nation is a great awakening. Only when God's people are in a revival will the nation be restored."

Leonard Ravenhill - "When the church becomes worldly, it is time for a revival. When the world becomes churchy, it is time for a reformation."

A.W. Tozer - "Revival is not just an emotional experience; it is a time of spiritual awakening that transforms individuals, families, and entire communities. It is a time when God's people are stirred to action, to reach out to the lost and to make a difference in their world."

What will bring about this revival to lead humanity and the world away from the brink of sudden destruction and annihilation? The answer is not finger-pointing or complaining but ***a new call to prayer for Fresh Fire upon the Church***. The spiritually sensitive cannot throw in the towel in surrender but respond to the promptings of the Holy Spirit with a sense of urgency.

Do not Just Complain; Act.

This rude awakening of gloom and doom confronting our world has led many, including born-again Christians, into frustration and anger to shower attacks and accusations on political leaders and those who do not see or believe the way they do. Even pastors and church leaders are becoming accustomed to using their pulpits to display their anger and judgment without offering hope or solutions to encourage their congregations to pray for a spiritual awakening.

Sadly, this attitude of some leaders has produced a new generation of Christians who quickly jump into criticizing and complaining mode instead of interceding for the Lord's intervention. It is almost like the enemy has set us up on the track of a blame game.

Though the gloom and doom of our day are rude awakenings to many, they have almost always preceded great spiritual awakenings. The Scripture and the Church's history bear witness that dark times of gloom and doom have often been the platform upon which many devout men and women of faith had bent their knees to seek the Lord for spiritual awakening and Fresh Fire in their day.

The prophetic sound from Isaiah is timely and telling: "Arise Jerusalem (people of God)! Let your light shine for all to see. For the Glory of the Lord rises to shine on you. Darkness as black as night covers all the nations of the earth, but the Glory of the Lord rises and appears over you. All nations will come to your light: mighty kings will come to see your radiance" (Isaiah 60:1-3 NLT).

The thick clouds of darkness would never be able to take over our world. The Spirit of the Lord and His Glory are upon the spiritually sensitive saints alert to His leading to impact the culture and its leaders. I believe this is God's hour to take His rightful place as the King of kings and the Lord of lords over the nations.

It is also the Church's hour to turn to the Lord for Fresh Fire, just as Scripture declares, "If My people who are called by My name will humble themselves, and pray and seek My face, and turn from their wicked ways, then I will hear from heaven, and will forgive their sin and heal their land" (2 Chronicles 7:14).

That is a divine prerogative that no other entity can exercise except His covenant people, the Church.

God's Dealings In The Past And Present

During the reign of the kings of Judah in the Old Testament era, they experienced seasons of renewal in their darkest hours of deep moral decay, despair, and apostasy. The revivals began with consecrated servants who were not afraid to declare the oracles of the Living God with prophetic voices to their generation, even at the cost of their lives.

Today, the Church is under intense satanic attack, encountering increasing moral and spiritual decline within its walls and the surrounding culture. Amid these cycles comes a new generation and a culture of apostasy, making many susceptible as easy prey to the WOKE ideology - **every wind of ideas contrary to the Biblical faith**. That sets the stage for cycles of decline and renewal, as evident in the past and present History of the Church.

Complacency and rejection of God's Word have come back to roost with humanity, incurring the woes prophesied by Isaiah, "Woe (judgment is coming) to those who call evil good, and good evil; Who substitute darkness for light and light for darkness; Who substitute bitter for sweet and sweet for bitter. Woe (judgment is coming) to those who are wise in their own eyes and clever *and* shrewd in their own sight! " (Isaiah 5:20-21 AMP).

Ultimately, the Sovereign Lord raises a new leadership that speaks to the generations, preparing them for the moving of the Holy Spirit. Could we be that new generation of spiritually sensitive leaders and believers in the Church and society today to intercede for Fresh Fire?

The spiritually sensitive cannot throw in the towel in surrender. The true Church must take its rightful place in the spiritual arena and respond to the promptings of the Holy Spirit with a sense of urgency. That is necessary to position the Church for the deep-shaking revival many have prayed for and longed for.

Let us explore how this bears out in Scripture and the history of revivals.

The Time Of Samuel

There was a gloom and doom of spiritual and social disillusionment among the Jews under Eli, Samuel's predecessor. Corruption ran deep in the priesthood and the nation. The sons of Eli, who served as priests and judges over the people, defiled the holy sacrifices with no regard for the things of God (see I Samuel 2:12-17, 29). Sexual immorality was running rampant among the priesthood. The Scripture says, "Now Eli was incredibly old, and heard all that his sons did unto all Israel; and how they lay with the women that assembled at the door of the tabernacle of the congregation. (see I Samuel 2:22). As a result, the prophetic voice of "Thus Says the Lord" was almost dormant or hardly heard.

During that time, Hannah interceded for a son whom she vowed and dedicated to the Lord's services. That son was the Prophet Samuel, whom the Lord raised to lead the nation out of the doldrums of apostasy into pure and unadulterated worship of the Lord.

Under Samuel's reign as priest and judge over Israel, the Glory of the Lord replaced the **Ichabod** (the glory has departed) that had engulfed the tabernacle worship during Eli's tenure. The gloom and doom ended with the dawn of a new era of spiritual, moral, and social awakening in Israel. That is how the loving God responded then and continues to respond when His people call on Him in challenging times.

The Time Of Christ

There were spiritual and social challenges in Israel during Christ and after Pentecost. According to Flavius Josephus, in his *Antiquity of the Jews, 50,* the Roman authority and the Jewish religious leaders of the day vilified the Word of God and persecuted the Church.

With the full force of Roman power behind him, Herod imprisoned John the Baptist and eventually beheaded him. That is no different from what many Christians are facing today. The political suppression under the Roman yoke, the corruption in the priesthood, and its consequent moral and spiritual decline among the masses had spilled over to every segment of the society.

The spiritually sensitive believers were alert to the promptings of the Holy Spirit during those dark times. Simeon and Anna, two devout individuals, vigilant and in tune with the Spirit, went to the temple at the appointed time for the dedication of baby Jesus. They recognized the **Kurios** moment of the Lord's visitation (see Like 2:25-40).

Let us take a peek through the corridors of past revivals for lessons on how devout folks in dark times sought the Lord for an outpouring of Fresh Fire to transform cultures. It has already begun in countries in Asia and Africa, where men and women earnestly seek the Lord through fasting and prayer for revival in their nations and communities.

The Wesleyan Revivals (1730s)

The spiritual condition in England before the Wesleyan Revivals of the 1730s was said to have been deplorable, decadent, and a cesspool. The formal Church of England was spiritually dead, and its priests did not preach the evangelical Gospel of salvation by grace through faith.

According to R. C. Ryle, Mr. Blackstone, a well-known English lawyer, went around the churches to hear every notable preacher in London. He reported after the visits that many of the Anglican priests were deists and did not believe in the Gospel. He remarked, "It was impossible to determine if the priests were followers of Confucius, Mohammed, or Jesus from their preaching."

Besides, alcohol abuse and crime ran rampant, with every sixth house on the block being a grogshop (a cheap bar where customers could get drunk on the equivalent of one penny). Violent gangs roamed the streets with impunity, terrorizing anybody outside after dark. They would disfigure people's faces with knives, stab people in the legs with swords, sexually assault women, and even murder while law enforcement was failing. Does that sound familiar?

The slave trade was at its peak and widespread with the support of the English aristocracy. In the eyes of those in power, human life was just a commodity to purchase and sell.

Against this background, young men like John, his brother Charles Wesley, and close friend George Whitfield refused to sit still and complain. Instead, they earnestly sought the Lord for an outpouring of His Spirit to awaken a morally dying nation. The revivals inspired and transformed a morally and spiritually bankrupt England.

Like the Wesleyan Revivals, past and present revivals continue to leave their marks of positive spiritual and moral transformation on the culture of the communities where they occur. It is worth noting that the Wesleyan Revivals contributed immensely to North America's spiritual and moral awakening and eventually ushered in the various religious awakenings that shaped the civil society of the United States. Whenever the Spirit of God is on the move, it leaves a trail of positive impact.

Businessman Prayer Revival - New York City (1857-58)

The United States in 1857, was on the verge of a potential civil war. The conditions in the major cities were bleak at best as the city dipped into a rapid spiritual and moral deterioration.

At the time, the United States was experiencing explosive population growth, with many immigrants flocking to New York City. Consequently, social tension and economic turmoil got out of control in the city. Exacerbated by the stock market's collapse, many business people were left desperate, empty, and looking for answers.

Unemployment and homelessness had become a growing problem for New York City, with over 30,000 men out of work. The situation in New York City today is not too different from before the businessman revival.

With a sense of urgency, Jeremiah Lamphier stood in the gap to provide spiritual solutions to the depraved city. He started a prayer meeting for businessmen in the North Dutch Church in New York City 1857. The prayer meetings quickly grew in popularity, with attendance increasing from forty people in just a few weeks to many thousands as the revival fire spread.

The meetings eventually sparked a wave of spiritual revival throughout the country. The Businessmen Prayer Revival offered hope and stability during the uncertainty and unrest. Just as Christ was the answer to New York's spiritual, moral, social, and economic woes, He is the answer to New York City and the rest of the world today. For the Scripture declares, Jesus Christ is the same yesterday, today, and forever" (Hebrews 13:8).

Yes, in the face of our overwhelming social and spiritual challenges - "CHRIST IS THE ANSWER (CITA).

The Welsh Revival (1904)

Before the revival, Wales was in a spiritual and moral decline. Many attended church services but as a tradition with little or no commitment to the teachings of Christ.

The majority worked in the coal mines for a minimum income, which they mostly spent on alcohol to the neglect of their families. Crime and violence had escalated as disillusionment gripped the community.

The leading ministers of the day did not sit back and complain but boldly preached the Word to challenge many to pursue spiritual things. Evan Roberts was among those challenged and stirred by the bold preaching of the leading minister of that era.

Roberts devoted himself to earnest prayer for awakening. As a spiritually sensitive believer, Evan Roberts prayed for over 11 years for a revival to transform Wales. The revival broke out in 1904, spreading throughout Europe and other parts of the world.

The outpouring of the Spirit transformed the spiritually and morally depraved society into the revival capital of that day.

According to the Welsh Gazette, whole cities came to Christ during the revival. Nightclubs and bars closed down, and the liquor industry incurred significant financial losses as a result of the mighty move of God, with their patrons turning away from alcohol to faith in Jesus Christ. The crime rate also decreased geometrically as the masses turned to faith in Christ.

The press report continued, "Crime had reduced to almost non-existent with the Police having no one to arrest, and judges idle with no cases to judge." Society had changed for the better in the wake of the revival.

The visitation of the Lord brought on such an intense spiritual hunger that many rushed to buy Bibles and other Christian literature till the stores ran out of them. Where legislation, laws, and decrees have failed, the name of Jesus is the only hope and trustworthy solution. Try faith in Christ; it always works because Jesus never changes (see Hebrews 13:8).

The Azusa Street Revival (1906)

The revival broke out during a deep racial divide in the United States. It was generally an eye-sore at that time to many to see blacks and whites in the same room, left alone worshiping together. A local newspaper in Los Angeles printed this disgruntled racist remark about the revival: ***An unhealthy intermingling of the races.***

Racial prejudice was visible in Los Angeles, like the rest of the country, as blacks and other racial minorities were oppressed and discriminated against by their white counterparts. Besides, a devastating earthquake in San Francisco impacted over a 300-mile radius, including Los Angeles, with economic and emotional distress. That weighed heavily on the minds of many in the Los Angeles area.

Amid the injustice and chaos, the Lord answered the prayers of His people, led by a one-eyed black man, a descendant of slaves, and a son of a sharecropper, William J. Seymour, to usher in the revival in 1906 on 133 Azusa Street in Los Angeles. The revival helped bring the races together and gave hope to a racially fragmented community suffering from the aftermath of an earthquake.

The revival fire torched many churches throughout the United States and beyond, spreading the Pentecostal/Charismatic Movement worldwide.

In the words of Dora, a 100-year-old saint (my beloved mother), "Revival fire burns the garbage out of our lives and communities to pave the way for seasons of refreshing so sweet and so pure to awaken the faithful."

Azusa East Revival – Dunn, NC (1907)

The Azusa East Revival demonstrated the power of the Holy Spirit to break down racial and cultural barriers. The revival, under the leadership of Rev. Cashwell, occurred amid a deep racial divide in North Carolina, barely nine years after the November 10, 1898, Wilmington Massacre of many African Americans by white supremacists. They destroyed and burned their homes and businesses. The damage and emotional wounds to the black community were so deep.

Hungry for the baptism of the Holy Spirit, G. B. Cashwell, a holiness preacher, arrived in Los Angeles to attend the Azusa

Street Revival meetings with great expectations. However, being a white preacher from North Carolina (then a racist state), Cashwell found mixing the races at a revival under a black preacher unacceptable and too much for his prejudice. He left offended because he could not see himself allowing a black man to lay his hands on him in prayer. Sadly, racial discrimination exists in the Church today, packaged in unassuming wrappers.

The Holy Spirit convinced Cashwell to repent and return to the meetings. Returning to the revival meetings, Cashwell went straight to the altar and prostrated himself in the dirt and sawdust, weeping and praying. William Seymour, the black pastor leading the revival, laid hands on the white preacher, Cashwell, and immediately received baptism in the Holy Spirit. William Seymour and his elders gave him an apostolic commission to take the revival message to the South.

G. B. Cashwell returned to Dunn, North Carolina, rented a vacant tobacco warehouse, and started revival meetings. The revival bridged the racial divide and brought healing to the wounds of the Wilmington massacre. That revival catalyzed the spread of Pentecostalism throughout the eastern seaboard of the United States.

Pyongyang – Jerusalem Of The East (1903-45)

As a closed society, North Korea did not allow outside influence on its people. Any contact with foreigners or adherence to Western (Christian) ideals was punishable by execution. The Korean monarchy had banned Christianity since 1758 and punished Christians with death. The Korean monarchy executed thousands of Catholics, including missionaries from France, in its last great persecution in 1866.

The underground Church did not sit back and complain, compromise, or leave quietly during the great persecution. The

Church saw it as a platform on which they bent their knees before the Lord for revival.

In 1882, When the United States established diplomatic relations with North Korea, the door opened for more missionaries to enter Korea. In 1884, the king of Korea granted Horace Allen, a Presbyterian missionary doctor, royal permission to evangelize after saving the life of a royal family member severely wounded during a coup attempt.

With that opened door, Presbyterian and Methodist missionaries from the United States and Catholic and Protestant missionaries from other countries went to Korea with the Gospel. Large numbers of Koreans responded to the Gospel message. By 1910, Korean Christians numbered over 200,000 in a nation of approximately 13 million. Prayer meetings erupted in homes and streets, with many Korean believers publicly praying and praising the Lord.

From Pyongyang, nicknamed **the Jerusalem of the East**, Christianity spread to China, Japan, Taiwan, and other nations in the region. That mighty awakening in Pyongyang earned it the converted name **Jerusalem of the East** by American missionaries. The revival transformed a brutal autocratic and death culture into hope for many in the region at the time.

The Hebrides Revival On Lewis Islands (1949-53)

The conditions before the revival suggest that the spiritual state of the Churches on the islands was stagnant and lukewarm. The churches were functional, yet their religious practices and traditions were carried out as duties and obligations rather than with a sincere, heartfelt desire for intimacy with the Lord. Their approach to the Word of God had become so legalistic, driving young people away from the Church.

As part of the school curriculum, students on the islands learned Bible stories, a short version of the Westminster

Catechism, and how to sing many Psalms. The students were also required to memorize the Ten Commandments and many other selected passages of scripture. Sadly, many Bible teachers in the schools on the islands had no personal relationship with the Lord. As a result, they made little or no spiritual impact on the youth.

The consequent spiritual drought on the island prompted Peggy, 84, who was blind, and her arthritis-disabled sister Christine, 82, to mobilize the churches into earnest prayer and intercession for revival on the islands. Peggy and Christine neither got into the blame game, finger-pointing, nor used their age and disabilities as excuses. Instead, they got into action to do something about the spiritual drought in their community.

How Do We Respond To The Challenges Of Out Time?

What must be the proper response to the challenges of our time? As R. A. Torrey rightly observed, "We do not see the power of God in the Church today because we are not desperate for it."

It all begins with spiritually hungry believers coming together to pray, seek the Lord, and talk to Him through HIS Word. That is the response of those desperate for the power of God. Our church programs could be uplifting and even edifying, yet they cannot substitute for earnest prayer and intercession for revival.

The gloom and doom of our world are indeed overwhelming. Still, the Church should not invest precious time in the blame game and finger-pointing at the world without offering solutions. Neither can the Church cut and run, leave quietly, or stay silent like an impotent institution of bystanders.

The Church is the divinely ordained agent that can turn things around. The Lord, therefore, declares, "You are the salt of the earth, but if the salt loses its flavor, how shall it be seasoned? It is then good for nothing but to be thrown out and trampled underfoot by men; "You are the light of the world. A city that is set on a hill cannot be hidden. Nor do they light a lamp and put it under a basket, but on a lamp-stand, and it gives light to all who are in the house. Let your light shine before men, so they may see your good works and glorify your Father in heaven" (Matthew 5:13-16). Now is the time for the Church to play its rightful role as the flashlight of truth to expose and dispel the works of darkness (see John 1:3:20).

We can accomplish much and see more happening as the Church taps into the power of prayer. In a remarkable statement, J. Hudson Taylor, a British Protestant Christian missionary to China, points the Church to the Lord's challenge, saying, "We are yet to test or try prayer power to its fullest capacity. If we want to see mighty wonders of divine power and grace wrought in the place of weakness, failure, and disappointment, let us answer God's standing challenge, 'Call to me, and I will answer you, and show you great and mighty things which you do not know.'"

That is a powerful means of inviting God's presence and revival into our lives and communities. In the most challenging time in his reign as King of Judah, Jehoshaphat did not sit back and complain nor turn to any human source for help. Instead, he mobilized the people of Judah to seek the Lord's help through prayer and fasting (see 2 Chronicles 20:1-5, 13).

God's power to save and revive His Church never eases nor diminishes. Our sins and spiritual weaknesses can create a barrier between us and God's presence, leading to a spiritual drought and a sense of distance from God. Still, we can turn to the Lord in prayer and rest assured in His rock-solid promise, "If My people called by My name will humble themselves, and pray and seek My face, and turn from their wicked ways, then I will hear from heaven, and will forgive their sin and heal their land" (2 Chronicles 7:14).

The loving God will surely visit us with an outpouring of His Spirit to awaken the lukewarm Church as we turn to Him in repentance. Let us prepare and position ourselves to experience and embrace the wind of the outpouring of the Spirit.

POSITIONING THE CHURCH FOR A VISITATION OF THE SPIRIT

For Zion's sake, I will not keep silent, and for Jerusalem's sake, I will not be quiet, until her righteousness goes forth as brightness, and her salvation as a burning torch - **Isaiah 62:1 ESV.**

The world has swayed further and further away from the divine order. For the most part, the leaders of this world's system see faith in Jesus Christ as an affront to their ungodly political agendas.

The postmodern mind condescendingly Views faith in Jesus Christ through the words of V. L. Lenin, the architect of Russian communism, that ***Religion is the opium of the people***. Thus implying Christians are a bunch of lunatics and brain-washed individuals *high* on religion and living on false hope, unable to think or reason for themselves. That is the lens through which the world's system and governments see and treat people of faith.

The decisions and policies of such governments impact both the righteous and the unrighteous alike. The Church must approach this dire situation as a corporate responsibility and mobilize the people of God to pray.

All the news stories in recent years show that history is heading toward an uncertain climax. That is causing a lot of fear and anxiety among the masses, even within the Christian community. That is impeding the onward march of the Church.

Amid the systemic pressure on the Church, the Lord promises, "For Zion's sake, I will not keep silent, and for Jerusalem's sake I will not be quiet, until her righteousness goes forth as brightness, and her salvation as a burning torch" (Isaiah 62:1 ESV).

For the sake of His covenant people, the Church, the Lord will not keep silent or still like an Egyptian mummy or a toothless bull dog. The Lord will intervene on behalf of His people. Despite our failures, the Lord still loves us and desires to forgive, heal, restore, and bring us into harmony as we repent (see 2 Chronicles 7:14).

Prophet Isaiah foresaw the loving God's desires to visit us amid the gloom and doom with a mighty outpouring of His Spirit: "Arise, shine; For your light has come! And the Glory of the Lord has risen upon you. For behold, the darkness shall cover the earth, And deep darkness the people; but the Lord will arise over you, and His Glory will rise upon you. The Gentiles shall come to your light and kings to the brightness of your rising. "Lift your eyes all around, and see: They all gather together, they come to you; Your sons shall come from afar, and your daughters shall nurse at your side. Then you shall see and become radiant, and your heart shall swell with joy; because the abundance of the sea shall be yours, the wealth of the Gentiles shall come to you" (Isaiah 60:1-5).

Therefore, let us not behave like the world walking mindlessly in thick darkness. We are children of light, prepared and ready to position ourselves confidently in anticipation of Fresh Fire from the Lord.

The Danger Of Becoming Like The World

Unless the Lord visits us with Fresh Fire and the Church is receptive to it, we stand in danger of encroachment from the world. That is a scary proposition and a nightmare. I pray that never happens.

In his brilliance and eloquence, John R. Mott captured what could happen if we sit idly back for the world to infringe on or encroach upon the Church, "The invasion of the Church by the world is a menace to the extension of Christ's Kingdom. In all ages, conformity to the world by Christians has resulted in a lack of spiritual life and a consequent lack of spiritual vision and enterprise. A secularized or self-centered Church can never evangelize the world."

Mott quite rightfully hit the nail on its head. The more the world invades the Church, or the Church tries to become like the world, the weaker and irrelevant it becomes. We cannot forget how the desire of the German Protestant Churches to get along or find acceptance with Adolf Hitler and the Nazis made many of them complacent in the torture and murder of millions of Jews in that country. That is a picture of a church "Having a form of godliness but denying the power thereof" (2 Timothy 3:5).

We must never forget that our true and only identity is in Christ and Him alone. Therefore, with all due diligence, may we ensure that our worship and praise are from hearts with burning desires to honor the Father.

That would require that the Word of God be our compass and rule of thumb in all matters and saturates us to live for the Lord. That will quicken us with a deep sensitivity to the promptings of the Holy Spirit to recognize the appointed time of His visitation – the **Kairos** moment. You might have missed other appointments, but this is one moment you do not want to miss as you position yourself for Fresh Fire from the Lord.

Awareness Of The *Kairos* Moment

As we anticipate an outpouring of Fresh Fire, we must remember that God operates in seasons or according to His ordained or appointed time, known as **Kairos** moments. Notice that Jesus told the disciples to wait in the Upper Room until they had received the promised Holy Spirit of the Father, specifying that it would not be many days from now (see Acts 14-5). That means there was a scheduled or appointed time for the Holy Spirit to come upon the disciples. Their responsibility was to wait for Him. The Scripture declares: "Now when the day of Pentecost fully came,.....they were all filled with the Holy spirit..." (Acts 2:1-4).

The Day of Pentecost was the appointed time or the **Kairos** moment, just as the Lord had planned. I still believe there is a divinely appointed timing for an outpouring of the Spirit upon this generation in ways we have never seen before.

It is, however, left for us to recognize the moment or the time of His visitation, the **Kairios** moment. The Lord sternly indicted Jerusalem for not realizing the **Kairos** moment or the appointed time of His visitation: "If you had known, even you, especially in this your day, the things that make for your peace! But now they are hidden from your eyes. For days will come upon you when your enemies will build an embankment around you, surround you and close you in on every side, and level you, and your children within you, to the ground. They will not leave in you one stone upon another, because you did not know **the time of your visitation**" (Luke 19:42-44). They did not know nor recognize **the appointed time** or the **Kairos moment** of their visitation.

Is the Church ready for a visitation of the Spirit of God? Luke's Gospel talks about two individuals, Simon and Anna, who recognized the **Kairos** moment of the coming of Christ into the world. They waited with expectancy and testified to its fulfill-ment (see Luke 2:25-39).

The prophets of old told of His coming. His Glory came in many **Kairos** forms and events, like the priesthood, the altar building, the temple, the appointed feasts, and the various sac-rifices. Finally, His bodily appearance in the person of His Son, Jesus Christ, who boldly declared, "He that has seen me hath seen the Father" (John 14:9). To the Samaritan woman at the well, He identified himself as the Messiah, saying, "I who speak to you am He" (John 4:26). To the Jews, he declared, "The Father and I are one" (John 10:30).

Despite all the evidence, the fulfilled messianic prophecies, and His statements, they did not recognize Him. John, the beloved disciple, solemnly reports: "He came unto his own, and his own did not receive him" (John 1:11). We need the Lord to sharpen our spiritual antennas and sensitivity to prepare for His visitation. He is about to unleash an unprecedented outpouring of His Spirit, and we must be ready for it.

That will require us sometimes to stop talking and remain silent in His presence to hear what the Spirit is saying or wants to tell us. As spirit-filled believers, we tend to want to do most of the talking. We have almost become verbal gymnasts, always talking instead of hearing the Lord's voice.

If we will only listen, we shall know what the Lord intends to do in our day. The Scripture contains abundances of promises from the Lord on His intentions to visit us with a mighty out-pouring of His Spirit. We must anticipate with unwavering faith like the early disciples did in the Upper Room (see Acts 1:1-4).

Scriptural Promises Of His Visitation

"And it shall come to pass afterward, that I will pour out my spirit upon all flesh; and your sons and your daughters shall prophesy; your old men shall dream dreams, Your young men shall see visions" - **Joel 2:28**

"For I will pour water on him who is thirsty, and flood on the dry ground; I will pour my Spirit on your descendants, and My blessings on your offspring; they will spring up among the grass as willows by the watercourse. 'One will say I am the Lord's'; another will call himself by the name of Jacob, another will write with his hand, 'The Lord's" and name himself by the name of Israel" - **Isaiah 44:3-5**

"Blessed be the Lord God of Israel, for He has visited and redeemed His people" - **Luke 1:68**

"You have granted me life and favor, and your visitation has preserved my spirit" - **Job 10:12**

"Through the tender mercy of our God; with which the Day-spring from on high has visited us" - **Luke 1:78**

We ought to be spiritually sensitive and alert to recognize **the Kairos moment** of His visitation, or we are due for indictment like the Jews when Jesus wept over Jerusalem, saying, "If you had known on this day, even you, the conditions for peace! But now they have been hidden from your eyes. For the days will come upon you when your enemies put up a barricade against you, and surround you and hem you in on every side, ... because you did not recognize the time of your visitation" (Luke 19:43-44 AMP).

We must watch out for specific indicators of readiness or anticipation for the Kairos moment or time of His visitation. Let us consider some of these indicators of alertness and sensitivity to what the Lord will do in our day.

Intensity in Prayer

The earnest prayer of the people of God almost always precedes revival or visitation of the Spirit. As A. T. Pierson put it, "There has never been a spiritual awakening in any country or locality that did not begin with united prayer. The effectiveness of the people of God to position themselves for a visitation of the Lord is measured by the intensity of their prayers." history is silent on any revivals that broke out without earnest prayer.

Sadly, many in the Church often talk about their longing for a visitation of the Holy Spirit but do extraordinarily little praying. Besides, many pastors and leaders speak much about prayer but do little of it themselves. That is not the right strategy for expecting divine visitation.

In his book **Revival Praying:** *An Urgent and Powerful Message for the Family of Christ,* Leonard Ravenhill wrote, "No man is greater than his prayer life. The pastor who is not praying is playing; the people who are not praying are straying. We have many organizers but few agonizers; many players and payers, few pray-ers; many singers, few clingers; lots of pastors, few wrestlers; many fears, few tears; much fashion, little passion; many interferers, few intercessors; many writers, but few fighters. Failing here, we fail everywhere."

Anticipating revival is not the time for complacency or excuses but for earnest and deep soaking prayers Recognizing the urgency of the times, Evan Roberts, the leader of the 1904 Welsh Revival, called for *bend knees* - a call for submission, humility, and intensity in prayer. That call was for then and for now. That is the key that unlocks the doors to the arena of an outpouring of Fresh Fire upon the Church.

Lillian De Fin, Smith Wigglesworth's granddaughter, shares a moving testimony about the power of prayer in the Democratic Republic of Congo, formerly the Belgium Congo, before independence from Belgium. Lillian was four years old when her parents served as missionaries in the Congo. They entered a remote village with the desire to evangelize the natives. The tribal leaders showed them a location under a giant cotton tree in the center of the village to set up their tent.

Unknown to them, lions gathered under the cotton tree at night to hunt the natives. Lillian's parents prayed earnestly after setting up their tent for divine protection and open doors to evangelize the natives. According to Lillian, there was severe thunder and lightning in the village that night, but it did not rain. Her parents were so concerned that they stood at the tent door praying for the Lords intervention and protection. Things calmed down, and they went to sleep.

The following morning, the tribal chief and his elders came to the tent door of the missionaries and said to them. "We want to know your God, for He saved you and our entire village from the lions." The Lord had answered the earnest prayer of the missionaries by turning what was meant for evil against them into a platform of opportunity to proclaim the Gospel. That led to the village's deliverance from lions eating their children and ushering in a revival throughout the surrounding communities. That is a powerful testament to the transformative power of prayer in bringing about spiritual awakening – a visitation of the Spirit.

Recognizing And Submitting To God's Sovereignty

The Lord operates according to His sovereign will, not our way or how we want things to happen. We must surrender our control and give God back His Church to have His way. We must let God be God.

Leonard Ravenhill remarked, "The most fierce hindrance of revival often comes from those in leadership who want to have control over the Church. They must yield to God's sovereignty amid revival's fire."

In conversations with pastors and leaders, I noticed many hold so fast to their denominational or congregational traditions and even elevate them into doctrines instead of the Scripture. That often perpetuates legalistic tenets of dos and don'ts that lead to control instead of positioning the people in God's grace for Fresh Fire.

Positioning themselves for Fresh Fire, the Early Church parted with the religious traditions that had entangled them in legalistic bondage. Their decision to walk in grace rather than the traditions of men drew intense persecution from the religious establishment of their day. The martyrdom of Deacon Stephen and Apostle James (see Acts 7:54-60, Acts 12:1-2), the threats against the disciples (see Acts 4:1-22), the imprisonment of Apostle Peter (see Acts 12:3-6), the relentless pursuit of the saints by Saul (Paul) before his conversion (see Acts 9:1-4), and Paul and Silas' unlawful arrest, torture and imprisonment at Philippi (see Acts 16:16-24) are but a few examples of the persecutions the early disciples experienced besides the Roman persecutions.

It is costly to turn away from the control of cultural and denominational traditions for the Lord to reign supreme in our lives and worship. Yet, the Lord must have His Church back as its Sovereign Lord. The early believers allowed God His rightful place as Head Of The Church and experienced a release of the Holy Spirit's power in the Upper Room on the Day of Pentecost. Consequently, persecution escalated as some disciples ended up in cages with lions, unarmed in amphitheaters against armed gladiators, burnt at the stake, and banished. The blood they shared was not in vain but became the seed for the tremendous growth of the Church.

It is because of God's sovereignty over the Church that the Holy Spirit to torchs it with revival fire and causes it to thrive, even amid trials and persecutions. However, the Church dwindles into irrelevance when mortal beings are at the helm and operate with humanistic ideas and traditions devoid of the power of the Holy Spirit. They have a form of godliness but denies the power thereof (2 Timothy 3:5 KJV). A word of wisdom, "Let us give God back His Church; for He is God without us, but we are nothing without Him."

Unwavering Obedience Of Faith

An unwavering **obedience of faith** implies obediently believing and responding affirmatively or in agreement to what God has said, done, and promised to do, even when circumstances on the ground or everything the eye sees suggest otherwise. It is believing and holding fast to God's promises against all odds. That means agreeing with the Lord despite one's condition or circumstances.

As was well put by Kathrine Kuhlman, unwavering **obedience of faith** is "When we stop believing what we see and start seeing what we believe." That kind of faith, according to Apostle Paul, "... calls those things which do not exist as though they did" (Romans 4:17".

Through their **obedience of faith**, the early disciples positioned themselves for the outpouring of the Spirit to serve the Lord (see Acts 2:1-2:1-4). They obediently and faithfully waited in the Upper Room for the outpouring of the Holy Spirit (see Luke 24:49 and Acts 1:4-5).

In the Old Testament, the Spirit came upon a select few, like kings, prophets, priests, and those the Lord chose to carry out specific tasks. It was, therefore, unheard of for ordinary folks like the early disciples to receive the Spirit. They grabbed hold of the promise through unwavering **obedience of faith**.

In like manner, they responded to the Lord's mandate of the Great Commission to carry the Gospel to every man's world (see Acts 1:8, Mark 16:13-18). By their **obedience of faith**, many followers of Christ have paid the ultimate price for their faith – martyrdom. That mandate of the Great Commission remains the same today for the Church. It is not a great suggestion nor great ideas or thoughts. It is the Lord's mandate to the Church, that still requires obedience of faith (see Genesis 4:20, Hebrews 11:6, Mark 11:224).

Unity And Not Division

Let me illustrate this point with my childhood experience. When I was 10, my parents sent me to my grandparents for the Christmas holidays. One morning, my grandfather took me to his cocoa plantation to show me some cocoa beans because I wanted to know where chocolate comes from.

On our way, I looked up and said to Grandpa, "Look, Grandpa, all the trees look the same and joined together." With a smile, Grandpa explained, "Son, they look the same from a distance, but as we get closer, you will see that they are all different shapes and sizes and separated." It was just as my Grandpa said when we got to the plantation. The trees were all different and separated. They were not the same.

Sadly, that is what the Church looks like from afar. However, as one gets closer, it becomes evident that the Church is divided on many grounds, including flimsy ones. Those who prefer hymns are looked down on by those who play contemporary music at their services. Others see themselves as spiritually superior to those without the Pentecostal experience. Some evangelicals dismiss liturgical services as anything spiritual.

It looks like we seek ways to divide or segregate ourselves, overlooking the fundamental truth that it is all about Jesus Christ and not us and our little groupings. The late civil rights leader, Dr. Martin Luther King Jr, observed, "The most segregated hour in the United States is Sunday morning." That does not speak well of the Body of Christ.

Unfortunately, we have allowed our denominational and church-group preferences to pump us into spiritual pride and prejudices against other blood-bought believers with whom we disagree. We must remember that it was in one accord or unity of purpose that the disciples gathered in the Upper Room for the most incredible release of Fresh Fire through the outpouring of the Holy Spirit (see Luke 24:39, Acts 1:4, Acts 2:1-4m, and Psalm 133).

The unity of the Church is so vital to our Lord that in His high priestly prayer, He prayed, "I do not pray for these alone, but also for those who [1]will believe in Me through their word; that they all may be one, as You, Father, *are* in Me, and I in You; that they also may be one in Us, that the world may believe that You sent Me" (John 17:20-21 see also Philippians 1:27)

The late Presbyterian pastor, Christian leader, missionary, and author, A. T. Pierson, re-echoed the essential nature of unity in the Church: "To a true child of God, the invisible bond that unites all believers to Christ is far more tender, lasting, and precious; and, as we come to recognize and realize that we are all dwelling in one sphere of life in Him, we learn to look on every believer as our brother, in a sense that is infinitely higher than all human relationships. That is the only way to bring the disciples together permanently. All other plans for promoting the unity of the Church have failed."

The phrase, *one accord* in the Book of Acts, depicts the magnetic power of unity to the revival of those days. That is much needed today to position ourselves for Fresh Fire. Unity is the breeding ground for revival; cherish it and thrive spiritually; reject it and scatter into the abyss of despair. That is wisdom to guide us in our spiritual pursuits today.

Adherence To The Fundamental Truths Of The Word

The fundamental teachings of Scripture are essential when positioning the Church for Fresh Fire. Unfortunately, some pulpits emphasize self-actualization, a human-centered ideology that exalts one's efforts rather than adhering to the sound teachings of Scripture. As a result, teachings on sin and judgment are no longer welcome and are put on the shelf in pastoral offices, collecting dust.

The word "sin" has virtually dropped out of modern church vocabulary. Denying the reality of sin, humanism and the so-called progressive thinkers contend that we are born **good** but sometimes make **bad choices**. That is a deceptive strategy to avoid the word, **sin**. The Scripture clearly states that sin is not just what we choose to do because it is a part of our human nature (see Romans 7:14-2:14-2). It is a genetic problem we must deal with through faith in Jesus Christ as long as we live (see Romans 7:25-8:1-3).

Even more disturbing and disheartening is the word **judgment** lays on the chopping block of Cancel Culture. Secularism, humanism, and WOKE ideology have infiltrated some pulpits to emphasize the God of love, and denying His judgment of sin. The same Bible that speaks of love also talks of judgment. While we may not like the thought of judgment or the consequence of sin, judgment is an unavoidable reality without faith in Christ.

Humanity is going deeper and deeper into a syndrome of everyone doing what is right in her own eyes (see Judges 17:6, 21:25). It is like playing baseball without an umpire. No new terminologies or changes in the language can ever change the reality of the consequences of sin (see Romans 6:23, 3:23).

The book of Nehemiah tells the story of the Jews who had survived 70 years of Babylonian captivity, returning to rebuild Jerusalem's burned and crumbled walls. As they gathered around one of the city gates, the scribe Ezra stood before the people and read from the book of the law of Moses. From morning till evening, Ezra stood on a large platform and read the Scripture aloud. He taught the Word with conviction and clarity.

As the people listened, they wept over their sins as "They stood in their places and confessed their sins and the wickedness of their fathers" (Nehemiah 9:2, NIV). They publicly acknowledged their sins and repented. In so doing, they positioned themselves for seasons of refreshing from the Lord.

Holding to the fundamental truth of God's Word provides a compass that directs the Church toward revival. It has the power to transform lives and renew spirits.

Emphasizing the transformative power of the Word of God, John Scott stated, "We must allow the Word of God to confront us, to disturb our security, to undermine our complacency, and to overthrow our patterns of thought and behavior."

The Word of God will change us and prepare us for an out-pouring from the Lord in these dark days. That would, however, necessitate an unwavering commitment on the part of the people of God to dedicate themselves to earnest prayer according to the Word and not just emotional outbursts of sounds from our larynx. It is a commitment with all hands on deck, solely focusing on the Lord, whose promises are yes and amen (see 2 Corinthians 1:20).

Yielding To Be Changed

To usher in a revival, we must be willing to pay the price of obedience. That means yielding every area of our lives to the Lord and aligning our thoughts, words, and actions with His Word, no matter the cost. That is crucial to make us available to the Spirit of God to quicken and transform us into channels and conduits of revival.

When we submit to be changed by the Lord, we become living testimonies of His grace and power, convicting and drawing others to Christ. That changes hearts and ignites a revival fire that spreads like wildfire in the hot Summer.

The price we must pay could sometimes mean life or death. Yet, it is needful for the Lord to use us. Leonard Ravenhill describes the cost in these words: "The cost of yielding to be changed by the Lord for revival is the crucifixion of self. It requires dying to our desires, ambitions, and ways of thinking and allowing the resurrection power of Christ to work in and through us."

The Welsh Revival was the Lord's answer to a simple but earnest prayer of total surrender of a young man, a yielded vessel, Evan Roberts, "Lord, bend me." In the Welsch language, it means "Lord, humble me." He desired to let the Lord have His way with him.

At age 13, Evan Roberts had a burden to pray for revival in Wales. For nearly 13 years, he prayed 4 hours daily from midnight to 4 AM for the revival of Wales. At age 26, the coal mines worker, with no formal ministerial training, became instrumental in bringing about that great revival -the 1904 Welsh Revival. Even Roberts was indeed a yielded vessel for the master's use.

In November of 1949, two sisters, Peggy and Christine Smith, 84 and 82 years old—Peggy completely blind, and Christine bent over with arthritis yielded to the Spirit of God to become the conduits of intercession on Lewis Island, paving the way for the Hebrides Revival of 1949.

Despite their age and failing physical health, Peggy and Christine were committed to paying the price of total surrender for the Holy Spirit to quicken them into vibrant intercessors who prayerfully mobilized the island to position them for revival.

The Lord is not looking for the most educated, influential, or the strongest to use. Instead, He seeks out those who make themselves available and yield in obedience to His purposes. Such are candidates for His use. Those are sensitive and alert to *the Kairos* **moment** of His visitation.

GOD'S SEVEN-FOLD PURPOSES FOR REVIVAL

---

*But now, for a brief moment, grace has been [shown to us] from the Lord our God, who has left us a surviving remnant and has given us a peg (secure hold) in His holy place, that our God may enlighten our eyes and give us a little reviving in our bondage. For we are slaves; yet our God has not abandoned us in our bondage, but has extended lovingkindness to us before the kings of Persia, to revive us to rebuild the house of our God, to repair the site of its ruins, and to give us a wall [of protection] in Judah and Jerusalem - **Ezra 9:8-9 AMP.***

This prayer by Ezra is the kind that opens the heavens for a release of Fresh Fire to awaken the Church, transform cultures, and change human hearts. It demonstrates Ezra's deep awareness of the Lord's mercy and grace towards them in spite of their past failures. That requires a shift in our thinking not to stay in the tombstones of our past failures but in the sufficiency of God's grace to move us into a refreshing season from the Spirit.

To Depend On His Grace: "...grace has been shown...."

The people of God had been in captivity, and their Babylonian captors had resettled pagans from other nations in their homeland. They went into captivity due to their disobedience and rejection of the Lord. In their state of disillusionment, the Lord showed them His grace by orchestrating their return home (see Ezra 1:1-11, Isaiah 44:26-28, and 45:1-4,13).

Ezra's prayer expresses his awareness of God's grace in allowing them back to Jerusalem to re-establish true worship. Our dependency on the grace of God is a recognition of our true nature as finite beings in need of divine sustenance. The Christian life is a journey of dependence on God's grace, not a performance to earn His favor. It is a life that is never possible without His grace.

In our performance-oriented culture, it is not uncommon to find believers seeking to accomplish or attain through works and performance what is only possible through grace and intimacy with God. Any human-made efforts to earn God's grace puts one into the bondage of dos and don'ts – into law rather than grace. The law demands and pressures its adherents to perform or produce works. Grace, however, provides peace and clothes the people in His righteousness (see Romans 5:19). Only God's grace can restore the Church into harmony and intimacy with Him for Fresh Fire in this darkness of apostasy and hopelessness.

Here is how the Lord conveyed His point to shift the mindset of Zerubbabel and the returned Jews from the works mentality to dependency on His grace and power, "This is the word of the LORD to Zerubbabel: 'Not by might nor by power, but by My Spirit,' Says the LORD of hosts. 'Who are you, O great mountain? Before Zerubbabel, you shall become a plain! And he shall bring forth the capstone With shouts of "Grace, grace to it!" (Zachariah:6-7).

Breakthrough and revival come not through performance, physical strength, societal status, or intellectual abilities but by God's grace and power. The awareness of His grace in our lives is the starting point in knowing and entering into divine purpose. Let us rely on God's grace because it is dependable.

The leaders of the Early Church never lost sight of the efficacy of God's grace. Apostle Peter's response to the Jews after the healing of the disabled person at the gate, Beautiful, makes the point, "You men of Israel, why are you amazed at this? Why are you staring at us like we had made this man walk by our power or godliness? The God of Abraham, Isaac, and Jacob, the God of our fathers, has glorified His Servant and Son, Jesus ⋯ And based on our faith in His name, it is the name of Jesus which has strengthened this man whom you see and know; and the faith which comes through Him has given him this perfect health and complete wholeness in your presence" (Acts 3:12, 13, 16 AMP).

Signs and wonders were common phenomena in the Early Church because Christ was allowed His rightful place as the King of kings and the head of the Church.

Apart from the grace of God, we are doomed, and humanity has no hope. When we realize that it is not by our power but by God's, we develop an awe-filled reverence for Him: That is true worship.

During the Walsh Revival, a reporter from the Welsh Gazette asked Evan Roberts, "How did it all begin?" He replied, "It is all about God; I always emphasized to the people to honor the Holy Spirit and let Him have His way with us." That is how we walk and live in His grace.

God wants to be honored and believed. It all comes together when He is moving among His people in revival. We do not need to go too far to grasp this truth. The fact that He saved us by His grace through faith settles the matter (see Ephesians 2:8-9).

To Preserve His Covenant People: "....God has preserved a remnant....."

God has always preserved a remnant to live and exalt His name in challenging times. The remnant here refers to the spiritual quality of men and women solely devoted to God's call. They are the ones who have survived the onslaught of the enemy, refusing to defile themselves with the filth of the WOKE world. The Lord preserves them to be conduits of the move of the outpouring of Hias Spirit among His covenant people - the Church.

Even in exile in Babylon and during the diaspora, when the Jews were scattered and almost on the verge of extermination, the covenant-keeping God intervened and preserved a remnant to return and rebuild the desolate places. In like manner, the Lord has established His Church on the earth to rebuild and restore the broken humanity and culture.

That is what the Lord did when King Ahab and his pagan wife Jezebel were persecuting and even killing the followers of God. Gripped with fear and self-pity, Elijah complained, "I have been very zealous for the Lord God of hosts because the children of Israel have forsaken Your covenant, torn down Your altars, and killed Your prophets with the sword. I alone am left, and they seek to take my life" (1 Kings 19:14).

Let us listen to the Lord's response to Elijah: "Yet I have reserved seven thousand in Israel, all whose knees have not bowed to Baal, and every mouth that has not kissed him" (I Kings 19:18). That was a preserved remnant plus Elijah himself whom the Lord preserved to usher in the spiritual awakening that brought the people back into harmony with Him (see 1 Kings 18:30-39).

In these dark hours, the Holy Spirit is awakening His preserved remnant. They are the willing vessels sold out to God to do whatever He desires of them, with them, and through them to make His name known all over the earth and among the nations.

Amid racial tension and economic devastation, a son of sharecroppers, a one-eyed African American, William Seymour, and his white friend, Frank Bartleman, and a small band of followers sought the Lord; they were the preserved remnants and conduits via which the Lord ushered in the 1906 Azusa Revival that spread the flames of Pentecostalism around the world. Though a few, they had a burning desire for revival.

Evangelist Billy Graham expressed the remnant's crucial role in challenging times: "In times of darkness and uncertainty, the remnant of faithful believers shines as a beacon of hope and light. Their unwavering commitment to Christ and His teachings is a powerful testimony to the transformative power of faith. Through the remnant, God works to bring about spiritual revival and renewal in the world."

You are a preserved remnant for such a time as this. Are you ready to take your place before the Lord for empowerment and instructions to make His name known? Remember, when hope seems scarce in the darkest days, even the slightest remnants of light can illuminate the dark tunnels of life to a brighter tomorrow. You and I could be that remnant of salt and light at this generation?

In total submission to the Holy Spirit, dedication to the Word, and fervency in prayer, the early disciples were the preserved remnant to impact their world with the Gospel of Christ. It is left for us to yield to the Spirit of the Lord to have its perfect will with our lives in these dark times in human history.

To Give Us Security: "**.....a secure place in His presence...."**

The Lord promises a secure place in His presence to people just coming out of captivity without permanent or stable residence. The Lord has an orchestrated plan to bring us to a place of stability, emotional and spiritual fortitude, and focus. As A. W.

Tozer affirms, "A revival is the renewing work of the Holy Spirit, drawing us closer to God's presence, where we find our ultimate security and purpose." Revival brings the Church to a stable and firm place of oneness in faith and spiritual pursuits.

In the Hebraic nomadic culture, **yāṯêḏ** (Hebrew for a peg) is used to hold down the cords to strengthen and secure a tent. The process of striking down the peg to secure the tent is **aman**, the Hebrew for **believe**. The Old Testament employs the verb **aman** 110 times, e.g., in Genesis 15:6. This linguistic correlation vividly portrays an unwavering devotion to God. Like a stake firmly embedded in solid ground upholds a tent in the face of a storm, **To have a nail or a peg in His presence** implies that we are entirely devoted to the Lord, and our thoughts and actions align with His Word, even in the most stormy circumstances.

The returned Jews were made secure in the Lord's presence to embrace His Word with unwavering devotion and faith. The outpouring of the Holy Spirit revives and places the Church in such security to align our thoughts and actions with His Word as a witness in a morally bankrupt culture.

The 1906 Azusa revival, at the time of a deep racial divide in America, brought William Seymour, an African American, and Bartleman, a white man, into such a secure place of intimate interracial friendship that infected the whole revival. That security repelled every suspicion that had swelled due to the racial tension into unity and stability in faith in Christ. They felt secure in the presence of the Lord, to the dismay of the racist culture of that day.

Their security prompted a local newspaper in Los Angeles to print its objection to the racial unity among the believers at the revival with the racist headline, **An unhealthy intermingling of the races.** That could not hinder the affinity among the races. It strengthened their unity and resolve because they were secured in the Lord's presence.

That revival was an opposition defying unity in a secure and safe place only found in the presence of the Lord. It was the Lord's doing and was marvelous in those days, and it would and should be for us, too, in our day.

To Enlighten Us: "....that our God will enlighten our eyes...."

In dark times, spiritual blindness overtakes humanity. Education and political ingenuity are incapable of removing the scales of blindness from the eyes of society; instead, they intensify it. The ineptness of the United States, Western Europe, and the United Nations is evident in their inability to bring about a peaceful settlement in the destruction of lives in the ongoing war in various regions of the world, including the Ukrainian-Russia war.

Chaos appears to spread like cancer around the glove. That indicates how a world without Christ could lead humanity into self-annihilation.

The lukewarmness and the inward focus of the Church are not helping either. The Holy God wants to open our eyes to discern what is happening in the spirit realm. He wants us to see what He is doing and what He wants to do. That is crucial because spiritual things are discerned spiritually (see 1 Corinthians 2:14), for "Surely the Lord God does nothing Without revealing His secret plan [of the judgment to come] to His servants, the prophets – His covenant people" (Amos 3:7).

The scales of blindness in the eyes of humanity and some circles of the Church are so thick and oppressive that we are losing our spiritual bearings and reference points. Consequently, our spiritual sensitivity to the things of God and alertness to the Holy Spirit's promptings are growing increasingly dull unless the Lord enlightens our spiritual eyes and sensitivity.

Many celebrate the Day of Pentecost as if it were all about speaking in tongues. It is more than that. When the day of

Pentecost came, the Lord filled the disciples with His Spirit and spiritual gifts of prophecy, word of knowledge, discerning of spirits, wisdom, and other spiritual gifts (see 1 Corinthians 12:4-11, Ephesians 4:11-16) to edify, enlighten, and guide them to recognize and confront the works of darkness.

May the Lord open our eyes to distinguish between good and evil, light and darkness, and sin and righteousness. Our God does not look on lightly when good and evil are equated in the lostness of humanity (see Isaiah 5:20). A true revival will take the blinders off the Church and enlighten us to discern the times and seasons, even the **Kairos moment** of His visitation. That is when we regain our sensitivity to the leading and promptings of the Spirit of the living God.

To Revive Us: " ... and give us a measure of revival .... "

Bringing us a measure of revival implies God ushering in changes in our circumstances, spiritual perspectives, and pursuits. The history of revivals shows that nations experience spiritual awakening after a major crisis like the great depression, political turmoil like a civil war, or a severe epidemic or natural disaster.

That was the case in Korea after the Korean War of 1950-1953. There was a mighty shaking and an infusion of the Spirit by the Lord to usher in the Korean revival. That was at the time when things seemed hopeless.

God will shake up and change things when He releases an outpouring of His spirit on the Church. Be careful not to stand in His way with our denominational traditions and churchy theology of when and how the Lord ought to operate. He is sovereign and does not need our vote or counsel (see Isaiah 40:13-14). The Lord will shake and even uproot those things not of Him (see Hebrews 12:25-27).

Through revival, the Lord brings His people out of darkness into the light of His amazing grace and love. Past revivalists attest to the chains of darkness shattered with a release of Fresh Fire through the Holy Spirit:

Billy Sunday: "When the Holy Spirit sweeps through the Church, the darkness of sin is swept away, and the brilliance of righteousness prevails."

A.W. Tozer: "Revival is God's way of saying to the world, 'Let there be light,' as the Holy Spirit breathes life into the Church, dispelling the darkness surrounding us."

Billy Graham: "The Holy Spirit's revival is a divine sunrise, scattering the night of despair and sin, bringing a new dawn of hope and salvation."

The Lord will never leave His Church in a rot. He will surely revive us when we are desperate for Fresh Fire, and pray as Prophet Habakkuk did: "O Lord, revive Your work amid the years! Amid the years, make it known; In wrath, remember mercy" (Habakkuk 3:2).

The Lord will answer our prayers for revival to awaken us to fulfill His ordained purposes for our lives and the nations. He will stir a new vigor and boldness in us to stand firm against the forces of darkness to proclaim God's goodness to draw souls into the kingdom. Thus, on the Day of Pentecost, ordinary folks, with renewed vigor through the power of the Spirit, proclaimed Christ and saw three thousand men besides women and children come to Christ in a single day (see Acts 2).

To Repair The House Of God: "....to repair the house of our God and the ruins...."

Throughout Scripture and the history of the Church, revival has always come to restore the things of God 9 sound doctrine and biblical worship) in their proper place and perspective in the

Church. Such repairs transform the lives of His people and the culture.

Evan Roberts, the leader of the Welsh Revival of 1904, observed, "Revival is when God's people come back to His Word, praying it into the life of the Church, and asking Him to accomplish His will." That is what repairing the House of God implies in this spiritual sense.

To repair His house – to restore truth and righteousness among His covenant people, the Lord calls for an intercessor to stand in the gap. With many pulpits today filled with WOKE pastors proclaiming a social gospel that rejects any teachings on sin and judgment, the House of the Lord desperately needs significant repairs.

Here is how the Lord describes the damage to His house and the need for significant repairs, "Her priests have done violence to My law and have profaned My holy things. They have made no distinction between the holy (sacred) and the profane (secular), they have not taught [people] the difference between the unclean and the clean, and they hide their eyes from My Sabbaths, and I am profaned among them. Her princes within her are like wolves tearing *and* devouring the prey, shedding blood, and destroying lives to get dishonest gain. Her prophets have smeared whitewash for them, seeing false visions and divining lies for them, saying, 'Thus says the Lord God'—when the Lord has not spoken. The people of the land have practiced oppression *and* extortion and have committed robbery; they have wronged the poor and needy and oppressed the stranger without justice. I searched for a man among them who would build up the wall and stand in the gap before Me for [the sake of] the land, that I would not destroy it, but I found no one [not even one" (Ezekiel 22:26-30 AMP).

Sadly, the Lord did not find any intercessors to raise the hedges and stand in the gap on behalf of the people. That indicates a lack of devotion and sensitivity to the promptings of the

Spirit of God. It also shows the numbness of the Church to the spiritual depravity of the culture.

With the family and society rapidly breaking down and lukewarmness encroaching on the Church, we need a spiritual awakening to repair and restore the House of the Lord. The Lord brings revival to restore truth and righteousness, which rebellious humanity has trampled underfoot through arrogance and deceit in the Church and the nations (see I Kings 18:30-39; see also Ezra 3:1-2).

With all the efforts of governments and the media to discredit and drag the Lord's name in the mud, could this be the season the Lord will release an outpouring of the Spirit to revive, repair, and restore His Church?

We need a great sense of urgency and desperation to pray as Prophet Isaiah did and ask the Lord to tear the heavens open and come down to help us. The spiritual drought is severe, and an outpouring from the Lord is the only way to reverse course. That will nourish the people of God and infuse them with zeal and fortitude against the enemy's devices.

To Protect Us: *".... To give us a wall......."*

When God comes down, He revives His people to protect them against the powers of darkness. Speaking to Moses, the Lord said, "I have, in fact, seen the affliction (suffering, desolation) of My people who are in Egypt and have heard their cry because of their taskmasters (oppressors); for I know their pain *and* suffering. So I have come down to rescue them from the hand (power) of the Egyptians ... " (Exodus 3:7-8 AMP).

God desires to raise the hedges around us in revival times so we do not lose ground to the enemy. However, when the walls of intercession break down, the people are exposed to relentless satanic attacks that impact the Church in many ways. With broken down walls or hedges:

- The destiny of the people of God is compromised (see Psalm 84:12).
- The people of God could experience a spiritual drain by the enemy (see Jeremiah 27:8).
- The people of God encounter continual satanic harassment (see Ecclesiastes 10:8).

However, intercession or hedge building can end the siege of Satan to bring freedom and deliverance to the people of God (see 2 Chronicles 20: 1-20).

Undoubtedly, intercession brought down the wall of division between East and West Germany. Desperate for divine intervention, persistent intercession led by Rev. Christian Further brought them victory. Through the intercession of the Church, led by Archbishop Desmond Tutu and many others, the Apartheid system in South Africa eventually came to an end with the release of Nelson Mandela from prison.

Let us raise the walls of protection around our families, communities, and the Church, for the Lord will cause us to bloom like beautiful roses after the sweet Spring rains; however, that attracts Satan's attention, placing us squarely in the enemy's crosshairs. Yet we have His rock-solid promise of continued presence (see Matthew 28:20).

Revivals In The Enemy's Crosshairs

Every divine agenda and purpose for humanity draws the enemy's ferocious attacks. God's plan to deliver his covenant people, Israel, from their Egyptian bondage saw the enemy's attacks manifested in the destruction of the male-born Israeli infants in Egypt. The birth of the Messiah, Jesus Christ, to deliver humanity from the tentacles of sin was no different. King Herod decreed the systematic destruction of Jewish babies, ages two and under, in Jerusalem and its surroundings. In all these cases, the enemy failed to thwart God's plans. Both Moses and Jesus survived the satanic onslaught to accomplish God's purposes.

Therefore, it should be no surprise to the Church that revival attracts the enemy's ferocious and relentless attacks because of God's purpose to restore and awaken His Church and transform the culture to save humanity from self-destruction.

Many revivals have seen intense persecution of their leaders as well as followers. The Early Church was severely persecuted by the religious leaders till the believers scattered outside of Jerusalem after the martyrdom of Deacon Stephen. Yet, they could not silence the Church ablaze with Fresh Fire (see Acts 8:1-7). Job declared the unstoppable nature of the purposes of God, saying, "I know that You can do all things and that no thought or purpose of Yours can be restrained or thwarted (Job 42:2 AMPC)

The Armenian revival that saw over 600,000 souls come to Christ in the Ottoman Empire (now Turkey) and Russia experienced intense persecution - torture and execution of about 1:5 million believers. That did not stop the saints from sharing their faith. They scattered into other parts of the globe, including Los Angeles, before the Azusa Street Revival of 1906.

Unfortunately, the Church has encountered much resistance and criticism from within. Also, the Church is sometimes resistant to the movement of the Spirit. The sad reality is that the Church prays for revival but resists it due to spiritual pride and prejudices if the manifestations are not as anticipated or through our denominational and church groupings. The Sovereign Lord chooses when, how, and the channel through which He rains His Spirit on the Church, but always for our benefit. The Lord does not operate according to our personal or sectarian agenda. The Church's resistance to the move of the Spirit is almost like we did not like the answer to our prayer for revival.

In his book, ***The Cross and the Switchblade***, David Wilkerson, the founder of Teen Challenge and the Time Square Church in New York City, wrote, "You asked the Holy Spirit for a miracle, and now that you've got one, you're trying to argue it away. People who don't believe in miracles shouldn't pray for them."

Ultimately, we can summarize God's purpose for revival in a straightforward sentence, "To awaken His Church and restore humanity into intimacy and harmony with Himself."

Let us not resist the move of the Spirit of Cod, but instead embrace it and yield to His promptings and leading to position ourselves for Fresh Fire. That is how we shall torch our marriages, families, communities, and churches ablaze for Christ.

THE CHURCH CANNOT BE SILENT

But Peter and John replied to them," Whether it is right in the sight of God to listen to you and obey you rather than God, you must judge [for yourselves]; For us, on our part, cannot stop telling [people] about what we have seen and heard — **Acts 4:19-20 AMP**

Ignatius of Antioch, an Early Church Father, warned the persecuted Church of his day, "Do not keep silent, for the voice of truth is the voice of God. Speak boldly, proclaim the Gospel, and let not the fear of men hinder you."

That applies to the Church today, especially in an era where the the political establishments and the WOKE Mob, with the backing of their Tech Giants allies, are trying everything to silence the voices of truth, the Church. All true believers in Christ must embrace Ignatius' warning like a badge of honor in their homes, communities, schools, workplaces, and every mountain of influence to live, exemplify, and proclaim Christ.

John G. Lake, who torched South Africa with the revival fire, reminds the Church, "Silence may be comfortable, but it is not what the Lord designed the Church for. The Lord has called us to be a force for change and renewal in the world." If the Church stays silent or leaves quietly to avoid confrontation with the world's system, it will cease to be relevant and impactful.

We must stay the course, proclaiming the uncompromising message of the Cross with boldness in the power of the Holy Spirit. That is how the Church will rescue the perishing and positively impact a crumbling society.

The opposite of impact is silence. The Gospel will not go out, and the lost will not find salvation if the Church retreats or remains silent. A silent Church makes no impact and sinks into irrelevancy. Therefore, any silence, retreat, or compromise on the part of the Church weakens its resolve and emboldens the enemy to hinder the Gospel.

The Liberian Experience

In the late 1980s, during the military rule in Liberia, the unlawful imprisonments and summary executions of political opponents and genocide against opposing ethnic groups went through the roof. Many politicians fled the country for their lives, leaving the masses at the mercy of the military government's brutality. The Church was under intense pressure from the military government to desist from speaking against their actions. They wanted the Church to stay silent.

However, after prayerful consultations, many pastors and believers jumped to the streets to peacefully express their disapproval of the government's actions. Some pastors, including me, were arrested and imprisoned for days and weeks with no end in sight, while the government agents secretly executed others.

Despite stiff opposition from the government, the pressure mounted by the Church continued till the message got across, and calm prevailed for some time.

As one of the pastors told me on the phone ten years later, "Brother Bobie, that show of strength by the Church during the military rule in Liberia is still having an impact." Any act of silence by the Church in the face of evil is in itself evil.

What would have happened had the Church in Liberia remained silent or left quietly? Let us not forget the pivotal role of the Church in bringing down the Berlin Wall in 1989 and the oppressive Apartheid Regine in South Africa in the early 1990s. The Church still has a vital role to play in the affairs of humanity.

Silence is the enemy of impact. In anticipating revival, the Church must never stay silent, leave quietly, or go into seclusion but instead stand tall and boldly proclaim, *Thus says the Lord.* We can either stand for something or nothing.

The Church: God's Vocal Watchman Over The Nations

The Church of Jesus Christ is the vocal watchman over the nations. William J. Seymour, the leader of the 1906 Azusa Street Revival, declared, "In challenging times, the Church must rise as a prophetic voice, fearlessly declaring the truth and exposing the lies. The Lord has called the Church to be the salt and light of the world, and our voice must not be silenced."

God has given the Church a divine mandate to hear and sound the alarms to warn the world to repent. If the Church stays silent as the world burns, the Lord will not look upon it lightly.

Here is the Lord's warning to a Church that neglects its responsibility to the world, "Son of man, I have appointed you as a watchman to the house of Israel; whenever you hear a word from My mouth, warn them from Me. When I say to the wicked, 'You will certainly die,' and you do not warn him or speak out to tell him to turn from his wicked way to save his life, that same evil man will die in his sin, but you will be responsible for his blood" (Ezekiel 3:17-18).

As the only hope for the world, the Church of Jesus Christ cannot allow itself to sit in oblivion, entangled in the cobwebs of fear, compromise, and silence. As God's watchmen over the nations, we cannot stay silent nor sit still as the world around us crumbles in despair.

To effectively carry out its responsibility as God's watchman and mouthpiece over the nations, we must be saturated in the Holy Spirit, always walking in wisdom and alertness and ready to face the forces of darkness when and where they lift their ugly heads. We better stay vigilant and firm in the faith, or the enemy will instill fear to silence the people of God. The Scripture warns, "Be sober [well balanced and self-disciplined], be alert *and* cautious at all times. That enemy of yours, the devil, prowls around like a roaring lion [fiercely hungry], seeking someone to devour" (1 Peter 5:8).

We Are Not To Leave Quietly

Acts chapter 16 tells of Paul and Silas, unjustly arrested, beaten, and imprisoned in a Philippian jail for the sake of the Gospel. Despite this injustice, they do not simply accept their release and leave quietly. Instead, they demanded that their rights as Roman citizens be respected and insisted on a public apology from the authorities, saying, "They have publicly beaten us without a trial and put us in prison—and we are Roman citizens. So now they want us to leave secretly? Certainly not! Let them come themselves to release us" (Acts 16:37 NLT).

That is a powerful demonstration of the people of God standing up for their rights and not allowing injustice to go unchallenged, especially when the world attempts to infringe on our faith. More importantly, that courageous stance by Paul and Silas gave the new believers in Philippi legitimacy and the courage to remain steadfast in the faith. Had Paul and Silas left quietly, the young congregation could have lost their confidence and faded into nothingness.

The Church should not go or leave quietly in the face of injustice or persecution. Doing so would only reinforce the view of some in the world that the Church is impotent and those in power can step on the people of God with impunity. Aimee Semple McPherson, the founder of the Four-Square Church and no stranger to pressure and attacks, lends these words of wisdom, "The Church should never leave quietly because our presence is a challenge to the status quo and confronts the powers of darkness with the transformative power of the Word of God."

The Church is a mighty moving force for positive change in a broken and corrupt world. That may involve speaking truth to power, exerting our spiritual authority through earnest prayer, standing fast on the Word of God, and taking legal action when necessary but never capitulating or leaving quietly. Many believers have experienced martyrdom for standing firm against unrighteousness, yet they never surrendered or compromised their faith in the face of death. A non-compromising Church is a shining light for spiritual and moral restoration in a world of deep darkness.

We Must Never Stay Silent

As a living organism, the Church takes its cues from the Lord, the Creator of the heavens and the earth, who declares He would neither be silent nor stay quiet until He restores His people, "For Zion's sake, I will not keep silent, and for Jerusalem's sake I will not be quiet, until her righteousness goes forth as brightness, and her salvation as a burning torch" (Isaiah 62:1 ESV).

We see that played out in the life of the Early Church when the Jewish authorities arrested and brought Peter and John before the Sanhedrin, the Jewish council of religious leaders. Peter and

John's offense was preaching and performing miraculous healing in the name of Jesus.

The council orders them to stay silent - to stop speaking about Jesus. But Peter and John replied, "Whether it is right in the sight of God to listen to you and obey you rather than God, you must judge [for yourselves]; For us, on our part, cannot stop telling [people] about what we have seen and heard" (Acts 4:19-20 NIV).

In such a powerful display of boldness, the disciples refused to remain silent despite opposition and persecution. Instead, they prayed for even much more extraordinary courage and confidence to continue preaching the good news of Jesus Christ (see Acts 4:24-31). The disciples' refusal to stay silent and their unwavering commitment to proclaiming the Gospel led to the growth and expansion of Christianity throughout the world.

The Gospel is only as effective as the Church commits to proclaim it. As an early American revivalist, Jonathan Edwards rightly affirmed, "The Church is to be a prophetic voice in society, and staying silent would be a failure to fulfill our divine mandate." That is a mandate the Church cannot compromise nor abandon.

The Church has so much to offer. Let us reject the world's philosophy that we must keep our faith at home or private. The world's system is trying to say that we are a nuisance and promises not to hurt or persecute us if we keep the Gospel of Jesus Christ far away from the public square. That is a trap to permanently silence the Church. There is no other way to stay relevant and influence the culture than publicly and privately sharing and living the Gospel message.

We Must Stand Firm To End The Drought

There is a divine call to action for the Church to stand firm and lead the way in ending the spiritual drought in the land: "Go, present yourself to Ahab (the world system devoid of hope and truth), and I will send rain on the earth" (I Kings 18:1).

The background of the verse is that the people had turned away from God and settled in absolute rebellion. They were experiencing the consequences of their actions - drought and despair. That was the physical and spiritual state of the nation of Israel when the Lord said to Elijah, "Go, present yourself to Ahab, and I will send rain on the earth" (I Kings 18:1)

To position the Church for Fresh Fire, God calls on the Church to take a firm stance to bring the people back into harmony with Himself. Taking a stand for the Lord attracts the enemy's relentless attacks on the people of faith. Yet, we must not lose heart but take encouragement from Tertullian, an Early Church Father and apologist who had experienced relentless persecution, "Hold fast to the faith and do not let go of the hope entrusted to you. The end may be near, but our resolve should be stronger than ever."

The Church is responsible as the light in the darkness to lead the way in a lost and broken world. By standing firm and holding fast to the truth, the Church can change the spiritual and moral drought plaguing the land. As we see in 2 Kings 18:39-45, when the people turn to God, He is faithful to forgive and heal the land with a torrential downpour of the Spirit to end the drought.

What would have happened had Elijah not stood before King Ahab and the people of Israel on Mount Carmel? With all its arrogance, the world system does not have the answers to the world's woes. No political or military genius can lead the world out of its self-imposed spiritual ad moral prison of darkness

The Church is the only divinely mandated agency qualified to take such a stand to bring humanity out of the darkness of dispair. What would become of our world if we failed to take a stand as a Church? The answer to this question is simple, "The revival that we have prayed and longed for could be delayed, and the carnage in the world would continue." Let us take a stand for righteousness now.

We Must Reject The Easy Way Out

Revival fire stays ablaze as the people of God stay the course and reject the easy way out. The Christian life is not an easy or comfortable expedition but a journey that requires endurance, sacrifice, and a steadfast commitment to following Christ. John Wesley, a revivalist of the 18th century, thus encourages the Church, "Revival requires an abandonment of self and total surrender to God's will. The easy way out only perpetuates the spiritual apathy that hinders the move of God."

The Scripture gives the Church a powerful example of rejecting the easy way out in the epic story of the three Hebrew *boys* in Daniel 3, who displayed an unwavering faith and commitment to God while staring death in the eyes. These three *boys*, Shadrach, Meshach, and Abednego, faced a difficult decision: bow down to King Nebuchadnezzar's golden image or face death in a fiery furnace.

Despite the immense pressure to take the easy way out by conforming, the three Hebrew *boys* refused and held fast to their faith in the God of Israel with this powerful statement, "King Nebuchadnezzar, we do not need to defend ourselves before you in this matter. If you throw us into the blazing furnace, the God we serve can deliver us from it, and He will deliver us from Your Majesty's hand. But even if He does not, we want you to know, Your Majesty, that we will not serve your gods or worship the image of gold you have set up" (Daniel 3:16-18).

What a fantastic display of courage in rejecting the easy way out by the 3 Hebrew *boys*. We lift the banner of the Cross higher and set the flames of revival ablaze when we resist the temptation of taking the easy way out - earnest prayer coupled with a radical abandonment of complacency and comfort births revival.

Choosing the easy way out stifles the flames of revival. We must stand our ground because the easy way out is Satan's deceptive trap that leads to emptiness, lukewarmness, and despair.

We Must Never Surrender Nor Compromise

There is a lesson in the 6th chapter of the book of Daniel for the Church to emulate - to resist any temptation to surrender or compromise the faith. Here is how Daniël's enemies hatched their diabolical plot against him.

They (Daniel's enemies) said, "We shall not find any charge against this Daniel unless we find it against him concerning the law of his God ...... When Daniel knew the king had signed the decree, he went home. And in his upper room, with his windows open toward Jerusalem, he knelt on his knees three times that day and prayed and gave thanks before his God, as was his custom since early days" (Daniel 6:5, 10).

The enemy knows when and how to strike a blow against the Church, but our God is never surprised. He will always sustain and protect His covenant people - the Church (see Isaiah 54:14-17). Our God will even make a way where there is no way (see Exodus 14:13-25, Joshua 3). Just as He did for His covenant people through the Red Sea and the Jordan River, He will do it again for His blood-bought Church.

Compromise is spiritual cancer that steadily eats away the integrity of our faith and renders us ineffective vessels for the Holy Spirit. Sadly, many leaders and believers, fearing persecution from the cancel culture mob and the WOKE media, have compromised to accommodate politicians in their pulpits to get along with those in power.

As a result, many see the Church as merely opportunistic, with its relevance as the umpire or referee over the moral and spiritual order in a society rapidly fading. The Church must prioritize obedience to God above all else and not seek to please the world, even when difficult or costly.

Let us consider some saints of old who refused to surrender or compromise their faith in the face of death, banishment, and excommunication.

Polycarp, Bishop of Smyrna (February 23, 155 AD)

Polycarp, Bishop of Smyrna and a disciple of Apostle John, angered the pagan community with a non-compromising declaration of Scripture that Jesus Christ is Lord. Consequently, a pagan mob in Smyrna, loyal to their pagan gods and Rome, demanded his life. The angry mob screamed, "Kill the church leader, and his church will die."

Refusing to compromise or recant his faith in Christ to save his neck, Polycarp made this profound statement before he was burnt at the stake, "For 86 years have I served Him, and He has done me no wrong. How can I blaspheme my King and my Savior?"

His shed blood was a seed for growth as his bold display of faith ignited a fresh awakening in Smyrna.

Martin Luther (April 18, 1521)

Martin Luther had the chance to recant his convictions and escape ex-communication from the Roman Catholic Church. However, fully persuaded by the truth of Scripture, he refused to compromise. In a remarkable display of courage and conviction, Luther delivered his non-compromising speech, first in German and then Latin, at the Diet of Worms on April 18, 1521. Resolute and giving an account of what and why he believed, Luther said,

"Unless I am convinced by the testimony of the Scriptures and by clear reason, I am bound by the Scriptures I have quoted. My conscience is captive to the Word of God. I cannot and will not retract anything since it is neither safe nor right to go against my conscience. Here I stand. I cannot do otherwise. God help me. Amen."

Luther's uncompromising stance resulted in the Protestant Reformation and the revival of the study of Scripture. We can always rest assured in the Lord's rock-solid promise, "I will never leave you nor forsake you" (Hebrews 13:5), when we stand for the truth. We are never alone; He is with us till the end of the age (see Matthew 28:20).

What would have happened had Peter and the apostles not stayed silent? What would have become of the Church in Philippi had Paul and Silas left quietly? What would have become of the modern Church had Polycarp and Martin Luther taken the easy way out?

These all stayed the course to pave the way for us to stay the course. If there is any time for the Church to stand firm and not leave quietly, it is now.

WE MUST DIE TO LIVE - PART I: THE QUADASH MOMENT

Yet indeed I also count all things as loss for the excellence of the knowledge of Christ Jesus my Lord, for whom I have suffered the loss of all things, and count them as rubbish, that I may know Him and the power of His resurrection, and the fellowship of His sufferings, being conformed to His death, if, by any means, I may attain to the resurrection from the dead – **Philippians 3:8, 10.**

The apostles and the members of the Early Church had an undeniable commitment to Christ and were willing to die for the faith. Indeed, some died, while others scattered across the region, but not quietly as they continued to declare the good news of the kingdom. The Scripture attests, "Therefore, those who were scattered wen everywhere preaching the Word" (Acts 8:4; see also Acts 11:19-25). They had purposed to die to self for the sake of the Gospel of Christ.

Paul expresses his willingness to die to *self* so that he might live for Christ, " ... For I am ready not only to be bound but also to die at Jerusalem for the name of the Lord Jesus" (Acts 21:14). That is a *"we must die to live"* moment. Such is a dedicated life set apart for the Lord - A sanctified life - *Dying to live.* That is a life set apart and totally sold out to the Lord without any reservations- ***The Quadash Moment.***

The Quadash (קָדַשׁ) Moment

The Scripture thus spells out the Quadash Moment, "Then Joshua said to the people, "Sanctify (Quadash) yourselves [for His purpose], for tomorrow the LORD will do wonders (miracles) among you" (Joshua 3:5 AMP.).

Dying to Live is what I refer to as the **Quadash Moment**, giving it all to the Lord for his purposes and glory. Quadash is the Hebrew for "to sanctify." In the Hebrew religious culture, whatever is sanctified or set apart is fully dedicated to the Lord with no reservations.

Unlike the English language, Hebrew writing is from right to left. Quadash comprises 3 Hebrew letters - שׁ ד ק. Let us look at these letters from their Ancient Hebrew pictographs and numerical values.

ק - The letter Qoof (ק) is represented by a picture of the back of a head or sunset. That implies the least or the last. It indicates the back of a person going or entering somewhere. Qoof has a numerical value of **100**, which signifies the **children of the promise.**

ד - The pictographic representation of the letter Dalet-ד is a doorway or an entrance that leads to a pathway. It's numerical value of **4** and signifies **creation or a new beginning.**

שׁ - The letter Sheen-שׁ is represented in the Ancient Hebrew pictograph with teeth; that means to **suppress, humble, or destroy**. Sheen has a numerical value of **300**, which signifies **the final blood sacrifice** made by the perfect lamb of God.

Thus, **Quadash - קָדַשׁ** implies that the believer who is the child of the promise enters into the pathway of a new beginning through the final blood sacrifice of the lamb of God to crush the world out of him for the Lord to transform him into a worthy vessel of use.

That is, indeed, Dying To Live - dying to the world into a newness of life through the blood of Christ and made into an anointed vessel worthy of His use.

One essential element when anticipating revival is our willingness to let the world die out of us. That is what the Scripture calls consecration or sanctification. Apostle Paul, thus, declared his **Quadash Moment**, "I am crucified with Christ; it is no longer I who live, but Christ lives in me; and the life which I now live in the flesh I live by faith in the Son of God, who loved me and gave Himself for me" (Galatians 2:20).

In his book, ***The Case of Discipleship***, Dietrich Bonhoeffer powerfully describes a life that is dead to the world and made alive and sanctified for the master's use :

"The Cross is laid on every believer. The first, Christ-suffering, which every man must experience, is the call to abandon the attachments of this world. Our encounter with Christ must result in the death of our old nature. As we embark upon discipleship, we surrender ourselves to Christ in union with His death — we give over our lives to die to self, that we might live unto Him. That begins at the Cross. That is not the terrible end to an otherwise god-fearing and happy life, but it meets us at the beginning of our communion with Christ. When Christ calls a man, he bids him come and die. It may be a death like that of the first disciples who had to leave home and work to follow him, or it may be a death like the execution of James and Paul, or it may be a death by burning at the stake like Polycarp, or it may be a death like John and Charles Wesley's, who had to leave the Anglican Church and go out into the world. It is the same death every time — death in Jesus Christ, the death of the old man at his call."

There is an urgent call to pray for revival. However, in doing so, We must be willing to die to the world for Christ to have His way with us. It must be *the Cross before us and the world behind us,* way of life. We cannot have a foot in the world and another in the Lord. He is either the Lord of all or not Lord at all. The Lord is not asking for a tithe or a tenth of our lives; He is asking for a hundred percent -what we are and shall ever become in Christ..

This higher calling in Christ is not a call to contribute but to surrender wholly to His sovereign will. We are either wholly in or not in at all. That was the implication when Joshua said to the people, "Sanctify – Quadash - yourselves, for tomorrow the Lord will do wonders among you" (Joshua 3:3). That is the formula to anticipate the move of God in the Church and our lives - sanctify ourselves.

Historical Event Illustrating The Dying To Abide (Live)

A historical account of the conquest of Mexico by Herman Cortez in 1519 sheds some valuable light on the concept of **dying *to love*.** Hernán Cortés arrived in the New World with six hundred men. Upon arrival, Cortés made an unusual decision - He destroyed his ships by setting them on fire. His strange action sent his men a chilling but firm message: ***There is no turning back. We are all in to finish the task of conquest.*** Two years later, he succeeded in his conquest of the Aztec empire. Cortés and his men all had a singular but superior goal: The conquest of the New World. They succeeded in their efforts.

To position the Church for Fresh Fire, we must ensure we are all in and not half-heartedly with alternative plans or a plan B in case things do not work out. We need to *burn the ships* of earthly attachments and say, like Apostle Paul, "Yes, everything else is worthless compared to the infinite value of knowing Christ

Jesus, my Lord. For his sake, I have discarded everything else, counting it all as garbage, to gain Christ" (Philippians 3:8 NLT).

That indicates that Apostle Paul is wholly sold out to the Lord. With the Cross before us, there is only a singular focus, a total surrender to Christ for His purposes. That avails us for the Master's use.

Sanctification: The Scriptural Concept of Setting Apart

is the divine process of consecrating individuals or communities for a sacred purpose. Sanctification in the Old Testament involved separation from sin and impurity, marked by ceremonial rituals and a commitment to follow God's commandments, with the ultimate goal of living a holy and pleasing life. This process is encapsulated in the Hebrew concept of "Quadash" (קָדַשׁ), emphasizing dedication and purification.

In the New Testament, sanctification takes on a more personal and transformative dimension. It represents the ongoing work of the Holy Spirit within believers, shaping them into the likeness of Christ. This process is characterized by progressive moral and spiritual growth, a deepening commitment to God's service, and the development of Christ-like character. Sanctification is not a one-time event but a lifelong journey of becoming more like Christ and living a life that reflects God's holiness and righteousness.

Through the Holy Spirit, sanctification positions the believer as a vessel for the Master's use. Thus, the believer is not of his own but of the Lord– *Dying to Abide (Live)* for Christ. It is all for His glory and Honor.

Die To Abide (Live)

I have been privileged to minister to hundreds of people at the altar at different churches in different states and countries throughout my ministry. I have seen many in tears, asking the

Lord to take over their lives and do whatever He desires. Many who pray such prayers are sincere and want to be vessels worthy of use in the Lord's hands.

Such was the heart cry of Charles Spurgeon, a great preacher of the Gospel. In his desire for Christ to be the all in all over his life, Spurgeon made this solemn remark, "I have now concentrated all my prayers into one, and that one prayer is this, that I may die to *self* and live wholly to Him."

If we desire a much closer walk with Christ, we must be willing to die to abide in Him. If we are not entirely all in, we deceive ourselves and do not abide in Him. As we position ourselves for Fresh Fire, we must surrender all we are and whatever we shall ever become to the Lord. That is the key to walking in His power and might.

Andrew Murray put it this way; "The deeper we are willing to enter into the death of self, the more shall we know of the mighty power of God and the perfect blessedness of a perfect trust."

Please note that the call to Christ is not a call to live but to die. How would you answer this question, "Are you completely sold out to God even to the point of your life, or partially in?'

That is like a question a military commander might use to evaluate his soldiers to identify those fit for battle. That determines our readiness for the move of God. Are you ready for what it costs to stay the course with expectancy for revival? Holy Spirit, help each reader of this book to come to that place where they can answer *yes* with certainty to the above question.

The True Story Behind The Hymn, "I Have Decided To Follow Jesus."

About150 years ago, in Northern India, a man named Nokseng embraced Christianity through the efforts of an American Baptist missionary. This decision stirred up the wrath of the village chief and the lead witch doctor. Summoning the villagers, the chief confronted Nokseng, insisting he renounce his newfound faith or face death. Standing firm, Nokseng declared, "I have decided to follow Jesus. No turning back, no turning back."

In the face of this resolve, the chief ordered the execution of Nokseng's two sons before him. The arrows swiftly ended their lives. Undeterred, the chief again implored Nokseng to recant, this time to spare his wife. Unflinchingly, Nokseng responded, "Though no one joins me, still I will follow. No turning back, no turning back." Tragically, Nokseng's wife met the same fate as an arrow struck her down. Even in the face of this anguish, Nokseng was resolute. For the final time, the chief offered him a chance to deny his faith and live, but Nokseng's conviction remained un-shaken. "The cross before me, the world behind me. No turning back, no turning back," he proclaimed.

Nokseng and his family were executed, but their sacrifice triggered a revival in the village. Profoundly moved by their un-wavering faith, the chief publicly confessed, "I, too, belong to Jesus Christ!" His confession ignited a chain reaction, causing the entire village to embrace a saving faith in Jesus Christ.

Nokseng's courage and faithfulness unto death is a loud, challenging call: "Will the true Church stand up and move away from what seems like an emotional feast packaged as worship into the business of the high calling in Jesus Christ?" The Chris-tian walk is a battle, and we must prepare for war. It is not a battle fought with bombs and missiles but a spiritual one that requires us to *die to self* and live wholly for the Lord. That is a life lived on a Budget of ***Dying To Abide (Live).***

Child of God, please remember that in your dying to self, you are never alone. What ever experiences to go through in the process, the Lord is there with you. The Psalmist declares, "Even when I walk through the darkest valley, I will not be afraid, for you are close beside me. Your rod and your staff protect and comfort me"(Psalm 23:4; see also Acts 7:54-60).

The Budget Of Dying To Liv

A life lived on the Budget of **Dying To Live** implies a consecrated life dedicated to honor and glorify the Lord. The components of such a life are what I have referred to as **Spiritual Budget**:

The Empty Tomb is a testament to the eternal future of those dead to self, while the Upper Room becomes a sacred space of communion and empowerment. Culminating in the Great Commission, this Budget guides believers beyond personal transformation, urging them to step into the world with the life-changing power of the Gospel.

The components of the Spiritual Budget weave a narrative of self-denial, resurrection power, and a relentless pursuit of the lost—a journey intricately connected to the heart of our Savior.

As Christians, a **Spiritual Budget** allows us to faithfully allocate our resources - spiritual gifts and talents to align with our commitment to Christ and His purposes.

As profoundly put by Dr. J. B. Danquah, a pioneer politician of Ghana; "We must die a little for others to live." That very much applies to the life of **Dying To Abide**.

If we are to see revival in our day, much more is required of the Church to follow the example of Christ: "Let this mind be in you which was also in Christ Jesus, ... He made Himself of no reputation, taking the form of a bondservant *and* coming in the likeness of men. And being found in appearance as a man, He humbled Himself .... " (Philippians 2:5-8).

A Challenge From An Old Saint

An old saint challenged me when I was ministering in Liberia as I gazed at his dimming eyes, listening attentively to his words of wisdom. He suddenly grabbed my right hand to get my undivided focus and, in almost a whisper, asked me, "Has your faith and dedication to follow Christ cost you anything?"

Before I could say anything, he said, "I do not need an answer now, but come back a week later with your answer." This old saint, Pastor David G. Kai, taught me through his living example and series of direct questions to equip me for the journey of ***dying to self*** to abide in Christ with love and dedication.

May I ask, "What has it cost you as you follow Christ?' Get to the secret place with the Lord and learn what *dying to abide* is about.

WE MUST DIE TO LIVE - PART II: THE COMPONENTS OF DYING TO LIVE

*"To be a Christian is to surrender not just our sins but our whole selves, holding nothing back. It is not just about dying to sin but dying to self." - **Andrew Murray.***

In navigating the diverse landscapes of our spiritual journey, the Christian life unfolds in chapters, each marked by profound truths and transformative encounters. From the humble Manger where our Lord embraced vulnerability to the sacrificial Cross that beckons us to deny self and the borrowed Tomb that declares His victory over death, our Spiritual Budget of **Dyi8ng To Abide** in Christ is a roadmap through the profound teachings of Scripture. The Empty Tomb is a testament to the eternal future of those dead to self, while the Upper Room becomes a sacred space of communion and empowerment. Culminating in the Great Commission, this budget guides believers beyond personal transformation, urging them to step into the world with the life-changing power of the Gospel. Together, the components of the budget weave a narrative of self-denial, resurrection power, and a relentless pursuit of the lost—a journey intricately connected to the heart of our Savior.

Budget Defined By Leading Economists
Ngozi Okonjo-Iweala - "A budget is a tool that helps us make the most of what we have and achieve what we value."

Joel Berg - "A budget is a moral document. It communicates in very real terms what we believe and value as a society."

As followers of Christ, our *Spiritual Budget* helps us to *prioritize* and efficiently utilize our spiritual gifts and callings in response to the promptings of the Holy Spirit to honor God. In so doing, we position ourselves for Fresh Fire to torch the world ablaze for Christ.

Let us explore the components of **Dying To Abide**, our *spiritual budget*:

Budget Of The Manger
Our Lord gave us a great example to follow. Though high and exalted, the Scripture thus states His dying to *self* when He took on the form of humanity, "Let this mind be in you which was also in Christ Jesus, who, being in the form of God, did not consider it robbery to be equal with God, but made Himself of no reputation, taking the form of a bondservant, *and* coming in the likeness of men. And being found in appearance as a man, He humbled Himself and became obedient to *the point of* death, even the death of the cross" (Philippians 2:5-8).

He owned it all, yet He was born in a manger. He came as a lamb of God (see John 1:29) and, therefore, was not born in a prenatal ward of a hospital or a palace but in a stable where lambs are born – in a manger. He humbled himself and took a lower status.

The Manger is not a place of honor and power. It is a place of vulnerability only to be cared for by the shepherd till eventually led into the slaughter. Our Lord, the Great Shepherd, cares for His own in the manger bosom of His unfailing love, grace, and mercy.

When dead to self and alive in Christ, we learn to live like Apostle Paul stated, " … for I have learned in whatever state I am, to be content: I know how to [be abased, and I know how to [abound. Everywhere and in all things, I have learned both to be full and to be hungry, both to abound and to suffer need. I can do all things through [c]Christ who strengthens me" (Philippians 4:11-14).

We do not seek wealth and status but are willing to be wherever the Lord requires. We have no honor to defend. Though we are lowly in status, He has entrusted us to proclaim Christ and Him crucified. Therefore, we no longer live for ourselves but for Him.

Budget Of The Cross

Our Lord satisfied the requirements of the law with a final blood sacrifice to usher in the New Covenant. Jesus admonishes anyone who wants to follow Him, saying, "If anyone desires to come after Me, let him deny himself, take up his cross, and follow Me. For whoever desires to save his life will lose it, but whoever loses his life for My sake will find it. What profit is it to a man if he gains the whole world and loses his soul? Or what will a man give in exchange for his soul?" (Matthew 16:24-26).

The Lord left His heavenly glory to take on the form of humanity to pay the penalty for the sins of all humankind (see Philippians 2:5-8).

The crucifixion or death on the Cross was Rome's way of humiliating, torturing, and suppressing all descent. Living by the Budget of the Cross demands that we go all the way for Christ, even giving our lives. It is a call of self-denial, putting Christ and His Cross first and foremost in all our endeavors.

Apostle Paul declared his commitment to go all the way for Christ, "But God forbid that I should boast, except in the Cross of our Lord Jesus Christ" (Galatians 6:14). He again states in Galatians 6:17, "From now on let no one trouble me, for I bear in my body the marks of the Lord Jesus." To Paul and the Early Church, the Cross was a badge of honor rather than a symbol of shame.

There is no other way to live by the Budget of the Cross except to go all the way in. As a 100-year-old anointed woman of faith (my beloved mother) often says, "If we are unwilling to take up our Cross, we are not ready and deserving to be called His disciples."

Zac Poonam captured the purpose and our call to take up the Cross this way; "God is looking for men and women who will never be content with mere experiences and "blessings," but who will take up the Cross daily and follow Jesus and thus manifest in their lives and their service the reality of those words, "It is no longer I, but Christ that lives in me." That, and that alone, is the Spirit-filled life."

That is the call to Christ: It is not a call to a picnic or a banquet but a call to die to *self* and live for Jesus Christ. Like a grain of corn, we must die to *self* to become productive or fruitful for His glory. That is the attitude of those anticipating Fresh Fire from on high.

Budget of The Borrowed Tomb

God provides for His people at the right time. The Budget of the Borrowed Tomb implies that He who created the universe owed nothing while He walked the face of this earth. He lived a selfless life with no bone of materialism.

In dying to *self* to be alive in Christ, we do not entangle ourselves with the things of this world, especially what the future holds. Our lives are safe and secured in His infinite wisdom; therefore, we need not consume ourselves with those issues. That is how we ought to live as the Scripture declares, "For to me (us), to live is Christ, and to die is gain" (Philippians 1:21). Either way, the Lord will care for His own - those dead to self and living for Christ.

Materialism is a thief of loyalty (see Matthew 6:4) and a revival quenching fluid. Many have focused on setting up for their earthly future rather than wholly trusting in the Lord. As a result, many have run into a shipwreck with their ministries. The devout servants of the Lord must focus on things above and unshackle themselves from unhealthy earthly attachments, which are a drag on our onward march to position ourselves for Fresh Fire. The dead does not concern itself with its final resting place. When we die to *self* and wholly sold out to the Lord, He determines the future. The Lord will never leave us hanging.

Budget of The Empty Tomb

A believer dead to self and alive in Christ lives by this fundamental truth that ***Jesus Christ holds the future, making our life of dedication and faithful anticipation of revival worth living.*** We do not stay still forever. Just as the grave or the tomb could not hold Him down, so also no forces or powers of this world can hold down His blood-bought Church.

The Church operates under a supernatural authority, the resurrection power. Throughout my ministry, the one thing the Holy Spirit reminds me daily is that without the resurrection of Christ, I have no gospel to preach and no hope for the future.

As R. C. Scroll pointed out, "The empty tomb stands as a stark reminder that nothing is impossible with God."

There is an eternal future for those who are dead to *self* to live for Christ. As beautifully put by Leon Morris, "The Cross is the victory; the resurrection is the triumph...The resurrection is the public display of the victory, the triumph of the crucified one."

Whether the saints are burnt at the stake, eaten by ferocious lions, dismembered by gladiators, or missing in action on the battlefield, it is not a permanent resting place. The Borrowed Tomb suggests no attachment, but the empty tomb indicates that it is temporary. The empty tomb demonstrates our glorious victory over death that awaits those of us who are dead to self and alive wholly for Jesus Christ. That is the sanctified living that positions the Church for Fresh Fire.

Budget Of The Upper Room

The Upper Room symbolizes a place of communion, fellowship, rededication, prayer, and empowerment (see Matthew 26:17-25; Acts 2:1-4). Living by the Budget of the Upper Room is walking in intimacy with the Lord. The Upper Room experience prepares the Church to submerge itself wholly into Christ, identifying with His death and readiness to give our lives for His name's sake.

The Upper Room is a secret place the child of God must desire with an unquenchable longing to be alone with the Lord for a revelation of His majesty and power. The disciples were with the Lord in the Upper Room for communion, fellowship, and dedication. Still, they returned there to behold the risen Lord and await power from on high — the outpouring of the Spirit on the Day Of Pentecost.

In an uplifting tone, encouraging believers to desire to be alone with the Lord, Jonathan Edwards stated, "There is no substitute for the quiet, daily communion with God that comes from spending time alone in a presence. It is in these moments that we are strengthened, encouraged, and transformed by His grace."

The ministry of the Church may be public, but the strength and power behind it come from being in a secret place with the Lord. To position ourselves for Fresh Fire, let us revisit the Upper Room (our secret place of prayer) to recharge our spiritual batteries snf keep the revival fire ablaze.

Here is what the Lord says about that power and its purpose, "But you shall receive power when the Holy Spirit has come upon you, and you shall be witnesses to Me in Jerusalem, and in all Judea and Samaria, and to the end of the earth" (Acts 1:8).

The Upper Room is not the final destination of the Church. It is, instead, a place of refreshing and renewal to carry the good news of the kingdom to all nations. The Upper Room, the site of Pentecost, is not the end but the refueling point for the Great Commission.

Budget Of The Great Commission

You must not keep standing at the Cross nor relax in your lazy boy recliner in the Upper Room to live in past glory: It is time to put on your boots and step out into the world with the demonstration of the power of the Gospel of Christ. In the Great Commission, the Lord calls the Church to die for others to live.

The Lord describes the challenges the Church might face while carrying out the Great Commission, saying, "Behold, I am sending you out like sheep among wolves; be wary *and* wise as serpents and be innocent (harmless, guileless, and without falsity) as doves. Be on guard against men [whose way or nature is to act in opposition to God], for they will deliver you up to councils and flog you in their synagogues. And you will be brought before governors and kings for My sake, as a witness to bear testimony before them and to the Gentiles (the nations). But you shall receive power when the Holy Spirit has come upon you, and you shall be witnesses to Me in Jerusalem, and in all Judea and Samaria, and to the end of the earth" (Matthew 10:16-18 AMP).

Despite the challenges, the Lord did not leave any wiggle room for argument, negotiation, or pick and choose concerning the Great Commission. At the same time, He has given us His rock-solid promise that He will be with us and never forsake us (see Matthew 28:20).

Hudson Taylor, the great missionary to China, reminds the Church, "The Great Commission is not an option to be considered; it is a command to be obeyed."

A genuine revival or spiritual awakening is never independent of the Great Commission. During seasons of revival, we receive Fresh Fire to set the world ablaze with the Gospel to rescue humanity from the tentacles of hell. Revival is not just for the believers to feel good or spiritually uplifted but also to go to every man and woman's world to declare the good news of the kingdom. Like *horse* and *carriage*, you cannot pick one and leave the other.

The Cross, the Empty Tomb, the Upper Room, and the Great Commission go hand in hand to draw the lost into saving faith in Christ. That is evident in Peter's first sermon on the Day of Pentecost (see Acts 214-41).

PRAYER: THE KEY THAT IGNITES REVIVAL - PART I

*.....for he is a prophet, and he will pray (**Palal**) for you, and you shall live* **– Genesis 20:7.**

Throughout the History of Christianity, prayer has always been the igniting force for revival and renewal within the Church. The earnest prayer of the Church has preceded every move of the Spirit since Pentecost.

Examples of this include the Reformation and the Wesleyan revival, which were born out of the prayer and fasting of their leaders. Despite all evidence on the power of prayer, it is sadly done less and less today in the Church. Even well-meaning pstors, leaders and believers who talk much about prayer hardly invest in prayer.

Leonard Ravenhill captured the lukewarm attitude towards prayer in the Church this way: "No man is greater than his prayer life. The pastor who is not praying is playing; the people who are not praying are straying. We have many organizers but few agonizers; many players and payers, few pray-ers; many singers, few clingers; lots of pastors, few wrestlers; many fears, few tears; much fashion, little passion; many interferers, few intercessors; many writers, but few fighters. Failing here, we fail everywhere."

It is, therefore, essential to explore prayer from its Hebrew roots and by the Principle of First Mention to discover its essence, nature, and true meaning. They help us capture the original intent of *prayer* when first mentioned or used in Scripture.

The *Palal* (פָּלַל) Moment

The first mention of prayer in Scripture was by God Himself in Genesis 20:7. In that context, the one in covenant with the Lord offers prayer to reverse what could become a devastating blow or harm to a people or nation. Thus, we pray for the Church, families, communities, and governments for deliverance, restoration, and renewal. That is a responsibility reserved for the people of God – the Church (see 2 Chronicles 7:14).

The Hebrew word for *pray* that God used in the passage is **Palal**, composed of 3 letters ל ל פ. Unlike English, Hebrew writing is from right to left. Let us explore the pictographic meaning of the three letters that make up **Palal – פָּלַל.**

פ(Pe) - In Ancient Hebrew, פ is represented by a picture of an **opened mouth**, implying **talking** or **speaking**.

ל (lamed) – In Ancient Hebrew, the letter ל is represented by a picture of **a shepherd's rod or staff**, signifying authority or instruction. In this case, ל appears twice in *Palal* (פָּלַל), signifying **ultimate authority**.

The pictographic meaning of פָּלַל - *Palal* suggests Speaking to the Ultimate Authority. God is the ultimate authority to whom those in a covenant relationship with Him can speak or bring their petitions. Therefore, because Abraham was in covenant with God, the ultimate authority, the Lord instructed Abimelech to let Abraham pray for him for deliverance and healing for himself and his people.

Abraham's Deception and God's Mercy

Abraham deceived Abimelech by presenting his wife, Sarah, as his sister to protect himself. Despite this, God intervened and prevented Abimelech from touching Sarah. The Lord then warned Abimelech: "Now therefore, restore the man's wife; for he is a prophet, and he will pray for you, and you shall live. But if you do not restore her, know that you shall surely die, you and all who are yours" (Genesis 20:7).

This raises important questions: *Why does God tell Abimelech to ask Abraham to pray for him? Isn't Abraham a liar and a cheat? Why would God use someone like him? Does God answer the prayers of a liar and a cheat?*

Max Lucado offers a profound response to these questions:"Our prayers may be awkward. Our attempts may be feeble. But since the power of prayer is in the One who hears it and not in the one who says it, our prayers do make a difference." In other words, the power of prayer lies not in the person praying, but in the One to whom the prayers are directed—God Himself.

Our Covenant Relationship And Prayer

Though Abraham was deceitful, his covenant relationship with God still granted him the righteous standing to intercede on behalf of Abimelech. The Lord had accounted righteousness to Abraham prior to his deceit: 'Abraham believed God, and it was accounted to him for righteousness" (see Romans 4:3 and Genesis 15:6) not by any works he had done but all by God's loving grace towards him. This highlights an important truth: it is not personal perfection but our covenant relationship with God that positions us to pray effectively.

"The effective, fervent prayer of a righteous man avails much" (James 5:16).

Several lessons emerge from Genesis 20:1-7:

1. Our covenant relationship with God supersedes our shortcomings. It is stronger than our failures or inadequacies.

2. This covenant relationship grants us the right to intercede on behalf of others, to turn back darkness, and usher in spiritual revival.

As we seek revival, it is through our covenant position in Christ that we can boldly approach God for a fresh outpouring of His Spirit in our lives, churches, and communities.

The Righteousness Of God Through Christ

Our covenant relationship with Christ gives us the righteousness of God. This righteousness is entirely about Christ and His finished work on the Cross:

"For He made Him who knew no sin to be sin for us, that we might become the righteousness of God in Him" (2 Corinthians 5:21).

Romans 5:19 also affirms this: "For as by one man's disobedience many were made sinners, so also by one Man's obedience many will be made righteous."

Our prayers bear fruit because of the righteousness we receive in Christ. As James 5:16 says, "The effective, fervent prayer of a righteous man avails much."

Therefore, we can expect our prayers for revival and spiritual awakening to be powerful and effective. We should not let our failures and shortcomings hold us back. Instead, we must depend on God's faithfulness. This does not excuse sin but instead emphasizes the need to trust in God's righteousness than being weighed down by accusations of failure. As believers, we must endeavor to keep short accounts with the Lord by confess and repent of our failures whenever the Holy Spirit convicts us of them. Now is the time to enter into fervent prayer for revival, trusting in our covenant relationship with God.

The Need for Revival in Our Time

In a world facing unprecedented levels of evil and satanic influence, a new wave of revival is desperately needed. Such a revival could bring about the social and political changes necessary to avert widespread destruction and calamity. Turning the tide of evil requires urgent action from the Body of Christ. We must ask ourselves: "Are we ready to put aside our divisions and differences, and unite in earnest prayer for God to tear open the heavens and pour out a fresh fire on the Church and the nations?"

It is time to embrace our identity as people made righteous through the sacrificial death of Christ. This is how our prayers can prevail: "The effective, fervent prayer of a righteous man avails much" (James 5:16). Let us unite in prayer, expecting God to move in a powerful way, knowing that He hears the prayers of those made righteous through Christ.

Prioritizing Prayer

Many ask, "Are we going to witness an earth-shaking, Holy Ghost-soaking revival in the world today?" The answer to this question lies in a renewed commitment to prayer. As Charles Spurgeon once emphasized, "We shall never see much change for the better in our churches in general till the prayer meeting occupies a higher place in the esteem of Christians."

While many often desire public ministry through teaching, preaching, and singing. The so-called church growth experts seek methodologies and strategies that are more often secular than scriptural. That is a misplaced priority. E.M. Bounds addresses this issue, stating, "The Church is looking for better methods; God is looking for better men... what the Church needs today is... men and women whom the Holy Ghost can use."

In these times, we must stop misfiring our spiritual weapons and recognize the specific issues that hinder the flow of

Fresh Fire in the Church. As Romans 8:26 and John 16:13 remind us, turning to the Holy Spirit in prayer is essential. The Spirit will show us the "what" and the "how" of our spiritual battles. Let us realign our spiritual priorities and commit ourselves to fervent targeted prayers.

Knowing and Targeting the Hold-Up

Our rebellion against God's order has brought His judgment. God, while loving, is also a God of justice. Sin has consequences, but repentance draws His mercy and forgiveness. The following passages highlight the gravity of our situation:

The Heavens Are Shut

"Or [else] the Lord's anger will be kindled *and* burn against you, and He will shut up the heavens so that there will be no rain and the land will not yield its fruit, and you will perish quickly from the good land which the Lord is giving you" (Deuteronomy 11:17 AMP).

That implies that rebellion against God creates a spiritual barrier that blocks or hinders our blessings. As a result, we cease to be fruitful and experience a rapid moral and spiritual decline.

The Heavens Are Shut

"Or else the Lord's anger will be kindled and burn against you, and He will shut up the heavens so that there will be no rain and the land will not yield its fruit, and you will perish quickly from the good land which the Lord is giving you" (Deuteronomy 11:17 AMP).

Rebellion against God creates a barrier that blocks blessings, leading to spiritual and moral decline.

The Heaven Over Us Is Stayed

"Therefore the heaven over you is stayed from dew, and the earth is stayed from her fruit" (Haggai 1:10 KJV).

When we reject God's order, the heavens close, and the earth becomes barren. Divine instruction fades, and hope dims.

The Heavens Are as Iron

"And I will break the pride of thy power, and I will make the heavens as iron and the earth as brass" (Leviticus 26:19–20).

When we disobey God, His displeasure blocks our experience of His glory and blessings. The sense of ICHABOD (the glory has departed) looms over us.

To break through, we must identify the spiritual barriers and target our prayers accordingly.**An**

Example Of a Spiritual Hold-up

God revealed a vision to me while ministering in a city where churches had opened and closed repeatedly. I saw a valley with homes and people, but it was overshadowed by the wings of a massive vulture, blocking the sunlight—the Spirit—from reaching the valley. That was the spiritual hold-up preventing revival.

When I shared this vision with local ministers, they turned to prayer. Before this, they had tried various strategies, but without prioritizing prayer, they saw no results. God made it clear: prayer must be the foundation of revival in that community.

The Scriptural Strategy

Scripture gives us a clear strategy for breaking spiritual blockades.

"Call to Me, and I will answer you, and tell you great and mighty things...which you do not know and understand" (Jeremiah 33:3 AMP).

"If My people who are called by My name will humble themselves, and pray and seek My face, and turn from their wicked ways, then I will hear from heaven, and will forgive their sin and heal their land" (2 Chronicles 7:14).

When the leaders in the valley prayed, the blockade lifted, and the Spirit of God began to move powerfully. As Jonathan Edwards said, "When God has something very great to accomplish for His church, it is His will that there should precede it the extraordinary prayers of His people."

Seeking Help Of The Spirit For Targeted Prayer

To break the strongholds in our churches and communities, we must ask the Holy Spirit for help. **Catherine Booth,** the wife of the founder of the Salvation Army, noted, "Through the Holy Spirit, our prayers become a mighty force for victory, breaking through strongholds and ushering in God's triumph."

The Spirit guides us in prayer, as Romans 8:26 affirms: "The Spirit...helps us in our weakness. We do not know what prayer to offer... but the Spirit Himself intercedes on our behalf." My wife and I have seen the Holy Spirit's power in our own family as we ask for His guidance in praying for our children.

Targeted prayers are vital to breaking spiritual barriers. Just as the heavens were shut (see Deuteronomy 11:17) and the sky withheld its dew (see Haggai 1:10), we must pray for the heavens to open and for a fresh outpouring of the Spirit as Prophet Isaiah did (see Isaiah 64:1-4).

Prophet Isaiah's Example

The Prophet Isaiah recognized the urgency of his time, praying specifically for his generation. He confessed, "For a little while, your people possessed your holy place, but now our enemies have trampled down your sanctuary" (Isaiah 63:18). This acknowledgment drew God's grace and intervention.

PRAYER: THE KEY THAT IGNITES REVIVAL - PART II

"Oh, that You would rend the heavens! That You would come down! That the mountains might shake at Your presence." — *Isaiah 64:1*

Throughout the history of the Church, earnest prayer has served as the heartbeat of every spiritual awakening, a force that transcends human effort and touches the divine. From the Upper Room in Jerusalem to revivals sweeping across continents, the fervent cries of the faithful have opened the heavens and stirred the hearts of countless souls. Through these humble yet powerful petitions, the Church has witnessed some of its most glorious moments, where the extraordinary flows from the ordinary and the sacred from the surrendered.

Prayer: The Key to Unlocking Revival

"Prayer is the key that unlocks and reveals faith. Effective prayer requires both an attitude and an action. The attitude is persistence, knowing we're in it for the long haul. We don't just seek a momentary flash of light; we strive to *be* that flash of light." — *Charles G. Finney.*

Every revival begins when the heavens open in response to the prayers of God's people. Through prayer, we invite an outpouring of His blessings to awaken the Church and transform nations. Our Savior never abandons His people, even in the darkest times and challenging circumstances. It was in a challenging time when Isaiah prayed for God to intervene on behalf of His covenant people. This prayer in Isaiah 64 is a heartfelt cry for God to open the heavens and come down in power.

R.A. Torrey once said, "The secret of all failure is our failure in secret prayer." If we cannot turn things around, we may not have taken the necessary faith-filled Action. In times of spiritual drought, we must pray for the heavens to open and for God's Spirit to saturate and revive us.

God has given His Church a strategy for opening the heavens through prayer. Isaiah 64:1-4 provides a prophetic blueprint for revival. Isaiah's prayer serves as a guide, teaching us how to pray effectively for revival and divine intervention. We must understand what to pray for and *how* to pray if we want to see God move in transformative ways.

Specificity In Prayer

In seasons of spiritual drought, our prayers must be specific. Isaiah's prayer wasn't vague; he boldly asked God to tear open the heavens and come down. "Oh, that You would rend the heavens! That You would come down!" — *Isaiah 64:1*

Specific prayers yield specific results. Revival leaders like William Seymour of the Azusa Street Revival in 1906 were clear in their prayers for the Holy Spirit's outpouring. Jonathan Edwards also emphasized the power of precision in prayer, stating,

"General prayers produce general results, but specific prayers unleash specific breakthroughs."

The heavens open when leaders are united and intentional in their spiritual pursuits. And just as the Azusa Street Revival broke cultural and racial barriers, we must pray for specific breakthroughs today.

Praying For Heaven To Open

Isaiah didn't ask for a mere messenger; he asked God Himself to come down and shake the world:

"Oh, that You would rend the heavens! That You would come down! That the mountains might shake at Your presence-- As the fire burns brushwood, As fire causes water to boil-- To make Your name known to Your adversaries, That the nations may tremble at Your presence! For since the beginning of the world Men have not heard nor perceived by the ear, Nor has the eye seen any God besides You, Who acts for the one who waits for Him" (Isaiah 64:1,2, and 4).

Today, the Church doesn't need new programs or trendy methods. We need God's presence to bring profound and life transfirnung revival. The world is in desperate need of a divine shaking. Only God's presence can overthrow the forces of darkness and establish His righteousness.

To Shake Tthe Mountains

"That the mountains might shake at your presence" — Isaiah 64:1

The mountains represent the challenges and obstacles that stand in the way of God's people. These are not just physical but also spiritual and societal strongholds that hinder us from experiencing His grace. When God comes down, He shakes these hindrances, just as He did at Mount Sinai in Moses' time.

Jonathan Edwards observed, "When the Spirit of God is poured out, it not only converts individuals but transforms entire communities." Revival reshapes the fabric of society, breaking down mountains of sin and establishing righteousness.

Some mountains are created by government policies while others are the sectarian traditions we have raised into doctrines that contradict Christ's teachings and mandate to the Church. When God visits His people, these strongholds crumble under the weight of His glory. As Charles Finney said, "Revival is a divine earthquake that shakes the foundations of societal mountains."

To BurnTthe Brushwood

"As a fire burns brushwood..." — Isaiah 64:2

When God visits His people, He purges the dead areas of our spiritual lives. Sectarian traditions and denominational divisions are burned away, allowing the Spirit to move freely.

Billy Graham once said, "Revival is a divine pruning process that removes the branches of falsehood and fear, allowing the Church and society to bear the fruits of righteousness and courage." God will expose and burn away the works of darkness, replacing them with His righteousness. Let me illustrate this point with an experience of the Christ Apostolic Church (CAC), the oldest Pentecostal denomination in Ghana.

The CAC Experience

In the heart of Bekwai, a city in the Ashanti region of Ghana, the Christ Apostolic Church (CAC), the oldest Pentecostal denomination in the country, confronted a community entrenched in fear. The grip of societal myths, demonic influences, and entrenched traditions had left both believers and denominational churches cold and indifferent. The pervasive fear emanated from a notorious two-story house, once a site for human sacrifices to ancestral spirits and gods. This house had become a source of haunting and terror for the community, leaving everyone on edge.

Undeterred by the ominous reputation of the haunted house, the Christ Apostolic Church took a bold step to evangelize the area. Surprisingly, the tribal elders, hoping to drive them away, provided accommodation in the very house filled with dread. Oblivious to the eerie atmosphere, the group followed their customary practice, spending three days and nights fasting and praying for divine guidance. On the third night, a 5-year-old girl revealed a vision where a man in a white robe assured them, "He will do it for you." That marked the inception of the powerful chorus, WOBE TUMI AYE AMA WO, signifying the assurance that God could overcome all challenges.

The divine intervention transformed the atmosphere in Bekwai. The Lord's visitation eradicated the darkness, fear, and anxiety that had plagued the town for decades. Establishing a local congregation in the city as their district headquarters, the Christ Apostolic Church became a beacon of hope, spreading the Gospel to surrounding communities.

As believers, the pruning process, though challenging, is essential for growth and vitality. Drawing inspiration from John 15:2, every branch in Christ that does not bear fruit is pruned to encourage renewed zeal and productivity. Just as an eagle renews itself through a meticulous process, believers must willingly undergo Christ's pruning to prepare for His purpose in these challenging times.

To Boil The Water: Magnifying The Lord Before His Adversaries

"As fire causes water to boil...to make Your name known to Your adversaries" — Isaiah 64:2

When God comes down, He reignites lukewarm believers and awaken unbelievers to His saving grace, just as fire causes water to boil, His presence causes the Church to rise with renewed strength, standing firm against the powers of darkness.

The miraculous intervention of God magnifies His name among adversaries. No power can withstand the name of Jesus, for "at the name of Jesus, every knee will bow" (Philippians 2:10).

The Miracle in Liberia

In the vibrant landscape of Liberia during the 1980s, I embarked on a divine mission to plant churches, and my journey led me to the heart of Monrovia, the capital city. There, in a mid-upper-class neighborhood, the seeds of a new church were sown. However, as the work of the Lord unfolded, a storm of opposition emerged from the community leaders, who, after a few months, not only resisted but threatened to have me arrested for imparting the Gospel to their children.

The catalyst for this resistance was the stark contrast between the newfound godly lifestyle embraced by the young people of the community and the lukewarm, often carnal behaviors exhibited by their parents. Faced with mounting opposition, I gathered the youth in prayer, seeking God's intervention. Divine intervention manifested swiftly when the lead instigator's girlfriend came down with a life-threatening appendicitis.

In an extraordinary display of faith, the ailing woman's daughter, a burgeoning church member, mobilized her peers to visit the house and pray for her mother's healing. With faith as their guide, they anointed her with oil, laid hands on her, and rebuked the sickness in the mighty name of Jesus. Miraculously, the woman rose from her bed, exclaiming, "I am healed, I am healed." This miraculous event not only astonished the community but became a turning point.

The tide shifted as those who once sought my arrest now sought prayer from me. The very parents who opposed their children's walk with the Lord now endorse and support it. The waters of opposition turned into a boiling fervor, and the name of the

Lord resounded, magnified by the transformative power of the Holy Spirit within the community.

As the harrowing Civil War gripped Liberia in the late 80s and early 90s, many churches succumbed to the chaos. Yet, the local church I had planted, fueled by the resilience and faith of its young members, not only withstood the storm but thrived. It not only weathered the challenges but birthed pastors and became a source for establishing numerous churches throughout the city.

Amidst the turmoil of war, the presence of the Lord silenced adversaries and elevated His name among the people. Today, that very church, born in adversity, is a testament to the enduring power of faith in God and the miraculous capacity for growth, even in the most challenging circumstances.

The Miracle In The Congo

Yes, every knee and every power of hell will bow at the name of Jesus. In the tumultuous 1940s, the daughter of the renowned evangelist Smith Wigglesworth and her husband embarked on a perilous mission to Belgium Congo, now the Democratic Republic of Congo. Their mission was to spread the message of faith and establish churches amidst the chaos of the war for independence. Faced with the constant threat of the Belgian military, local freedom fighters, and a climate of fear, the missionary family found themselves in a remote village, assigned a spot beneath a towering oak tree by the tribal chief.

Little did they know that the seemingly chosen spot harbored danger, as it was a gathering place for lions at night, posing a lethal threat to the villagers. Unbeknownst to the missionaries, the tribal leaders had strategically placed them there, hoping the lions would eliminate them. However, a miraculous event unfolded as they prayed for divine protection and the grace to impact the community that night. Thunder and lightning filled the night, driving away the lions and securing the safety of the missionaries.

This extraordinary manifestation of divine intervention became a turning point. The tribal chief and elders, recognizing the power of the God of heaven, approached the missionaries the next day, confessing their sinister plan. The villagers were astounded by the protection granted that night because they had lost children to the lions. The incident paved the way for the adversaries to embrace the missionaries, leading to a profound transformation within the community. The Gospel flourished, and the impact of the couple's mission work, supported by their little daughter, resonates in the nation today. It is a testament to the unstoppable nature of God's plans, echoing the words of Job, "I know that you can do everything and that your plans are unstoppable" (Job 42:2 GWT).

When they call on Him in prayer, the Lord covers His people with a protective shield. Even the enemy's devices will turn into a platform for the Gospel will impact the world.

Divine Action: *".... Who acts for the one who waits for Him!"* (Isaiah 64:4)

The Lord has great delight in acting on behalf of those who, through faith, have trusted and patiently wait on Him. Those who wait on Him have received empowerment (see Luke 24:49, Acts 2:1- 4), ministry directives (see Acts 10:9- 48, Acts 131-3), and deliverance of the saints (see Acts 12:3- 17).

Prophet Isaiah summed it this way, "But those who wait for the LORD [who expect, look for, and hope in Him] Will gain new strength *and* renew their power; They will lift their wings [and rise close to God] like eagles [rising toward the sun]; They will run and not become weary, They will walk and not grow tired" (Isaiah 40:31 AMP).

Indeed, the Lord intervenes to protect and deliver His own. There are abundant testimonies of God's protective care and deliverance in every hut, village, town, city, and nation where people worship the Lord in spirit and truth. The past and modern history of the Church and the nations attest to that.

A historical but unfamiliar example to many believers is the powerful manifestation of the power of God in bringing down the Berlin Wall. That event was in response to the earnest prayer of intercession by some faithful believers in Germany. The fall of the Berlin Wall is nothing short of a supernatural miracle.

As John Wesley, a leader in the Wesleyan Revivals, declared, "Prayer is where the action is." More than that, prayer triggers a chain reaction in the spirit realm to bring down strongholds.

Miracle Of German Reunification

In the annals of history, many attribute the fall of the Berlin Wall to the resounding words of President Ronald Reagan. Yet, the profound narrative of Germany's reunification delves deeper. It unveils a powerful testament to the divine intervention that transcends political speeches and policies. Beneath the shadow of the oppressive East German Communist Party, led by the iron fist of dictator Erich Honecker, the German Democratic Republic (GDR) enforced draconian control, casting a pall of fear over those who dared to defy their regime.

Amidst this grim backdrop, a humble Lutheran priest, Reverend Christian Führer, ignited a spark of hope that would eventually blaze into an inferno of change. Five years before Reagan's historic declaration, Rev. Führer initiated the "Prayers For Peace" movement, a weekly congregation seeking divine intervention to dismantle the Wall and unite a divided Germany. Initially dismissed by authorities, the prayer meetings blossomed into a massive gathering, attracting thousands. Undeterred by spies, intimidation, and job losses, Pastor Führer and his follow-ers persevered, their faith unwavering.

The pivotal moment arrived on October 9, 1989, culminat-ing seven years of steadfast prayer. Pastor Führer led a peaceful prayer walk in Leipzig, with over 100,000 Germans bearing lit can-dles. In a breathtaking display of unity, soldiers, initially armed and ready, found themselves disarmed by the peaceful resistance of their compatriots. Russian tanks, once formidable symbols of oppression, rolled away. Within weeks, the communist dictator, Honecker resigned, and Soviet leader Mikhail Gorbachev initiated dismantling the Berlin Wall. The miraculous events of that Octo-ber night were the true catalysts, affirming that divine interven-tion, manifested through the people's courage, led to Germany's reunification.

The narrative of Germany's reunification goes beyond polit-ical maneuvering; it is a testament to the extraordinary power of faith, courage, and the miraculous events that transpire when the people of God come together in prayer. Rev. Christian Führer's un-wavering commitment, alongside thousands of believers' peaceful but prayerful resistance, demonstrated that nothing is impossible with God. The fall of the Berlin Wall was not merely a geopolitical shift but a profound revelation of God's extraordinary power, working through the hearts and actions of His people.

The Hebrides Revival on Lewis Islands

In 1949, the Lewis Islands were on the brink of spiritual and moral despair, a condition that deeply troubled two elderly and disabled sisters, Peggy and Christine Smith. Peggy, 86-years-old was blind, and her sister Christine, aged 82, was cripple with arthritis. Recognizing the urgency of the situation, these devoted women dedicated themselves to seeking divine intervention for their Barvas village church. Their tireless intercession unfolded in the quietude of their cottage, where two to three nights a week, from 10 PM to 3 AM, they fervently prayed and waited on the Lord for a revelation of His outpouring.

After weeks of unwavering commitment, Peggy experienced a profound vision—a crowded church filled with young people and an unknown minister preaching. Prompted by this divine revelation, she urgently summoned church leaders, including her pastor, to join in regular prayer sessions every Tuesday and Friday night. The sisters continued their simultaneous prayers, setting the stage for a divinely orchestrated movement that would reshape the spiritual landscape of the Hebrides islands.

The enthusiasm of their intercessory prayers sparked a desperate seeking of God for revival among ministers and believers alike. Unfazed by the harsh winter conditions, they gathered in unheated buildings, praying earnestly with a conviction that God had instructed them to "ask for revival." This collective cry led to the arrival of evangelist Duncan Campbell at the Barvas Free Church, marking the beginning of the Hebrides Revivals. The intervention of God was palpable as He delivered, protected, and revived His people, showcasing the power of unified, earnest prayer within the Church—a manifestation of Fresh Fire from the Lord.

The gloom and doom of our world have stirred up a rude awakening in the hearts and minds of many. The responsibility of the blood-bought Church is to call on the name of the Lord as Isaiah did for His intervention. Indeed, when the Lord comes down, the powers of darkness crumble, and the people find healing, restoration, and deliverance in His presence. The mighty shaking of His presence unshackles humanity from the tentacles of darkness. Certainly, the Lord will visit us if we call on Him.

Throughout history, God's interventions have testified to His power. From the Azusa Street Revival to the fall of the Berlin Wall, we see that when people call upon the Lord in prayer, He acts in ways that defy human understanding.

Waiting On The Lord

Isaiah 64:4 reminds us that God acts on behalf of those who wait for Him. In prayer, we receive strength, guidance, and deliverance. Whether in personal battles or national crises, God has always been faithful to act when His people wait upon Him in prayer.

As John Wesley declared, "Prayer is where the action is." Through prayer, we invite God's divine Action, shaking the heavens and earth to reveal His glory and revive His people. Let us call upon the Lord, trusting He will come down and shake the mountains in our lives, communities, and nations.

SETTING THE CULTURE ABLAZE
WITH REVIVAL FIRE

Then the high priest arose, and all those with him (the sect of the Sadducees) were filled with indignation and laid their hands on the apostles and put them in the common prison. But at night, an angel of the Lord opened the prison doors and brought them out, and said, "Go, stand in the temple and speak to the people all the words of this life – Acts 5:17-20.

Throughout history, God has often used difficult circumstances—such as persecution, death, and imprisonment—as tools to bring His people together and foster spiritual awakening. The early disciples were frequently imprisoned (Peter in Acts 12:5-11, Paul and Silas in Acts 16:19-34) or martyred (Stephen in Acts 7:54-64, James in Acts 12:1-2), yet their unwavering faith inspired others to believe and spread the Gospel even further.

The Sovereign Lord's Unconventional Methods

The Lord often brings His people together in the most un-expected ways and places. The Scripture illustrates how God uses strange and unusual circumstances to achieve His purposes. In the Old Testament, the story of Joseph stands out. Though he was sold into slavery by his brothers, falsely accused, and im-prisoned, God ultimately used these hardships to elevate Joseph to a position where he could save his family and many others from famine.

In Acts 5:17-20, we find a unique record where all the apostles were simultaneously imprisoned. But God's plans tran-scended their confinement.

Amid growing persecution, many saints and leaders fled to regions beyond Jerusalem. Yet, it was in a prison cell where the apostles found themselves together—perhaps for the first time in a long while. Their shared suffering ignited a fire for the Lord that couldn't be extinguished, as seen in other instances like Daniel 3, Daniel 6, and Acts 16.

That was our experience during the Liberian Civil War in the late 1980s and early 1990s; pastors and leaders faced re-lentless persecution, including systematic arrests, for speaking out against the abuses of the brutal regime of military dictator Samuel Kanyon Doe. With violent crimes, ethnic killings, and the suppression of dissent, communication was nearly impossible due to the lack of access to phones. Pastors often could not meet to strategize or even support one another.

Remarkably, it was during our arrest and imprisonment by the military government that we experienced a rare moment of unity. In the cold, windowless cell, we gathered for the first time in months and held one of our most spiritually fulfilling prayer sessions. Instead of praying for deliverance, we praised God, find-ing unexpected strength and peace while awaiting an uncertain fate.

Ten years later, in late 2000, one of the pastors who was in prison with me on a phone call said, "Brother Bobie, the impact of our prayer time in Moronvia prison is still felt today in the city."

Could the Church today need a similar encounter to bring us together? In a current church environment where denominational and racial divides run deep, what will it take to unite the Body of Christ and set the culture ablaze for His glory? Must we wait for a great persecution before seeking the Lord as one?

The Angelic Keynote Speaker

While the apostles sat in that dark cell, an angel appeared with a life-altering command from the Lord: "Go, stand in the temple and speak to the people all the words of this life" (Acts 5:17-20). That wasn't a gentle suggestion—it was a divine directive.

The apostles were no longer in fear. That prison became their conference room, where the angel delivered a keynote address - God's instructions clearly and powerfully. God united and empowered His people in that unlikely conference room for the task ahead.

Standing Together in Unity

The angel's message was clear: ***"... go and stand."*** It was a call to overcome fear, doubt, and self-pity—to stand together as a united body. There is power in unity. A divided church cannot change the world. The strength of our message, conduct, and attitude must reflect our unity, as Jesus prayed, "... that they may all be one, just as you, Father, are in me, and I in you."

Throughout Scripture, unity is essential to the Church's strength and influence. Psalm 133:1 echoes this truth, "Behold, how good and pleasant it is when brothers dwell in unity!" The blessings of unity are profound—King Solomon wrote in

Ecclesiastes 4:9-12 that " ... two are stronger than one, and a threefold cord is not easily broken."

Yet, today's Church is more divided than ever. Denominational pride has splintered us. **Andrew Murray** said, "The unity of the Church is not in uniformity, but in harmony; not in organization, but in fellowship; not in dogma, but in Christ." We must find common ground in Christ, where unity of purpose drives us to transform the world for His glory.

As **Charles Finney** rightly states, "The church can never become what it should be until unity becomes a consuming passion within her." The Church's mission is clear: we must prioritize unity to fulfill our calling and bring the Gospel to the nations. The Puritans got it right in their approach to Church unity, "Unity in essentials, liberty in non-essentials, and clarity in all things."

Knowing the Location

The angelic message was location-specific: *"... to the temple."* This location mattered. The temple was the epicenter of Jewish community life – religious, social, and political. Therefore, preaching there would ensure the Gospel reached the people. The world often tries to silence the Church, pushing it to the sidelines of societal discourse. But the Church must engage with culture and be present in every arena—government, media, education, and beyond.

The Lord calls us to go where His light is dim and His voice not hardly heard. As an evangelist, I've learned that obedience to God's direction, especially regarding location, is not always easy yet fruitful. The correct location is critical to the impact of our ministry, just as it was for the Early Church. The apostles' missionary journeys, like Paul's to Macedonia (Acts 16:6-10), were divinely guided and location-specific, each place serving as a launchpad for the Gospel to spread far and wide.

The Lord has anointed and commissioned His Church not only for friendly territories but also to unfriendly and hostile settings as well. The Lord called David Livingstone to Africa, far away from his native Scotland. He ministered among natives, who were often hostile and resistant. He and his wife shined the light of the Gospel in what was considered a dark continent then. They paid the ultimate price for the Gospel – they died in Africa.

Many believers in Christ have suffered similar fates as they responded to the leading of the Spirit. Yet, still, their sacrifices were not in vain. As Tertullian, an early Church father, apologist, and theologian, argued in his work *Apologeticus*, Christian martyrdom, instead of destroying the faith, only led to its further spread with this fantastic quote, "Semen est sanguis Christianorum," meaning "The blood of the martyrs is the seed of the Church." – Every drop of a martyr's blood is a seed for growth for the Gospel.

The Target Audience

The angel's command focused on ***"the people"***—the community in the temple. Similarly, Jesus' Great Commission (Matthew 28:20) sends us into the world to reach everyone with the Gospel. The Church's mission is to bring the Good News to everyone regardless of race, gender, culture, or status. Salvation is for all people – everyone is a candidates for salvation.

Understanding the target audience is crucial to effectively communicating the Gospel. That doesn't mean a WOKE ideology, a social gospel, or compromising the message for political correctness, but tailoring it to resonate with the hearers' worldview, just as Paul did on Mars Hill in Athens (Acts 17:22-34).

We must overcome cultural barriers and prejudices, ensuring the Gospel remains relevant and Impactful in every context. Only the unadulterated Gospel of Jesus Christ can reach the depth of our depravity and the ends of the human race.

Faithfully Proclaiming the Good News

The angel's directive was to proclaim ***"all the words of this life"***—the whole Gospel. We must be faithful to this mandate, not allowing denominational biases or cultural preferences to dilute the message. As the world-renowned evangelist **Billy Graham** said, "The Gospel has never changed; it is still God's power to save and transform lives." Our focus must remain on Christ crucified, the only hope for the world.

History has shown that revival comes through faithful preaching of the Gospel. The great revivals—New York's Prayer Revival, the Welsh Revival, and the Azusa Street Revival—were birthed from prayer and bold proclamation, not through political agendas or social programs.

Too many voices are competing for the world's attention, and yet cannot solve the overwhelming challenges humanity faces. The only hope for the world is the Gospel of Christ alone.

Staying in Tune with the Holy Spirit

To sustain revival, the Church must stay attuned to the Holy Spirit. Jesus promised in John 16:13 that the Spirit would guide us into all truth, and Acts 1:8 reminds us that the Spirit empowers us to be His witnesses. The Holy Spirit's promptings lead us to the right people, places, and moments to impact the culture.

The early Church experienced this firsthand. Philip's ministry in Samaria and his encounter with the Ethiopian eunuch (Acts 8:26-39) were Spirit-led moments that transformed lives. Peter's outreach to Cornelius (Acts 10:35-48) broke cultural barriers and expanded the Church's mission. That experience at Cornelius's house well-positioned Peter to help the Early Church in their decision to support Barnabas and Paul's outreach into the Gentile world (see Acts 15:6-11).

The Cost of Obedience

Following the Holy Spirit isn't without cost. Like Stephen, James, and Paul, many faced imprisonment, suffering, and even death for their obedience. Yet, through their sacrifices, the Church continued to spread the Gospel and sustain the fire of revival across cultures and nations.

Let us remain in tune with the Spirit, discerning the times and boldly proclaiming the Gospel. The world is waiting.

KEEPING THE REVIVAL FIRE BURNING

And they continued steadfastly in apostles' doctrine, fellowship, breaking bread, and prayer. Then fear came upon every soul, and many wonders and signs were done through the apostle ... So continuing daily with one accord in the temple and breaking bread from house to house, they ate their food with gladness and simplicity of heart, praising God and having favor with all the people. And the Lord added to the Church daily those who were being saved — **Acts 2:42, 44-47.**

True revival stirs the souls of lukewarm believers and awakens spiritually and morally bankrupt communities. Despite its significant positive impact on society and people, the gains gradually fade away. That is particularly so when the excitement settles and people cease to follow the Word of Truth. As a result, they plunge into an even greater darkness than before. The natural consequence is abandoning the path they once zealously pursued.

Revival Fire: Why Does It Flicker Out?

I was, therefore, not too surprised when a precious, spirit-filled elderly lady, a few years ago, approached me with this question: "Why is it that after a season of revival, communities often seem to revert, plunging into even deeper spiritual and moral decline?"

That is a question that should stir the hearts of every believer, especially pastors and leaders. The problem after revival is that people too often begin to live on the memory of past experiences. They hold themselves in the shrines of past glory, neglecting the work of maintaining the flame through consecration, and soon fall into a worse state than before. Others also resist the new workings of the Holy Spirit.

That still rings true today. Too often, I have attended church services where speakers focus on titles and past identities, bragging, "I am a Pentecostal," for spiritual superiority, rather than faithfully holding fast to the Word of truth and in prayer to sustain the revival fire. They linger in the memories of past revivals, clinging to former glories instead of embracing the fresh movement of the Holy Spirit and His current work in the Church.

The Nature of Spiritual Warfare

I responded to the dear lady with this thought: "A revival doesn't stop Satan from working against the Church. He works even harder during a revival, waiting for the Church to let down its guard."

Indeed, revivals have brought about significant transformations in communities, but an intense spiritual battle always follows with a bull's eye on the backs of believers. To infiltrate, the enemy looks for cracks—moments of complacency and division. Without vigilance, the fire of revival can be extinguished, leaving communities vulnerable to a deeper moral and spiritual decline.

Take, for example, Pyongyang. Once called the "Jerusalem of the East" due to the revival from 1903 to 1945, it is now under one of the world's most oppressive and brutal dictatorships with a systematic onslaught on the Christian faith.

New York City, the scene of the Businessman Prayer Revival (1857-59), is now a city of spiritual and moral filth with rising murder rates and criminals walking around with impunity. It is worse today thsn before the Businessman Prayer Revival.

Los Angeles was the site of the Azusa Revival of 1906, credited for spreading the Pentecostal/Charismatic Movement worldwide. The revival transformed Los Angeles into a vibrant city of moral and spiritual richness. The city is almost a war zone, becoming a den for murderers, criminals, drug dealers, and people with addiction and homelessness.

The same goes for Canada. The nation of Canada, the site of the 1994 Toronto Blessings, a revival that touched the world with Fresh Fire, is now dwindled into lukewarmness and rapidly escalating into a political, social, and moral cesspool. Why is that? The answer is not hard to find. - Complacency on our part.

The Danger of Spiritual Complacency

As **Billy Sunday** warned, the fire of revival is extinguished when we quench the Holy Spirit through complacency, compromise, overconfidence, and a lack of fervor in pursuing God's presence. Consequently, the revival fire in the Church fizzled.

When the Church becomes complacent, we neglect essential spiritual disciplines like prayer, dependence on the Holy Spirit, and commitment to biblical truth. Worldly distractions dim the flame of revival, and internal conflicts sap the energy needed to keep the fire burning. Without vigilance, the Church shifts its focus from radical faith and supernatural manifestations to institutional or denominational routines. When that happens, Satan seizes the opportunity to bring destruction, as Jesus warned in Matthew 12:43-45.

A Call to Vigilance

The solution is clear: "Be sober, be vigilant; because your adversary the devil walks about like a roaring lion, seeking whom he may devour (1 Peter 5:8)" The Church must remain in step with the Holy Spirit to sustain revival and keep the forces of darkness at bay. We are the earth's salt and light, preserving truth and righteousness and keeping the enemy from taking ground.

A Blueprint for Sustained Revival

Thankfully, God has not left us in the dark. He has given us the blueprint for keeping revival fire ablaze, found in Acts 2:42: "And they continued steadfastly in the apostles' doctrine, fellowship, in the breaking of bread, and in prayers."

It all centers around the Word - the teachings of Christ, fellowship around the Word, sharing and breaking bread through communion and generosity, and earnestness in prayer according to the Word. That is a simple but winning strategy that never fails. Let us explore the Early Church's plan for sustaining revival in Acts 2:42.

The Power of the Word of God

The Word of God is the foundation of every revival. The Early Church anchored itself in the teachings of Christ, not swayed by cultural trends or subjective opinions. They held fast to the objective truth of Scripture.

Revival cannot happen without the **Word**. As **Charles Finney** said, "The Word of God is like a fire that consumes the dross and ignites the hearts of believers, sustaining the fire of revival." **Jonathan Edwards** echoed, "Revival is not sustained by human effort alone but by the power and authority of the Word of God." Church tradition or discipline may benefit the congregation but is not a recipe for sustaining revival fire. God's Word stands alone.

The Church must stay grounded in the Scripture to keep the revival going. . The Scripture testifies that "While Peter was still speaking these words, the Holy Spirit fell upon all those who heard the Word" (Acts 10:44). Faith comes by hearing the Word of God (Romans 10:17), and faithfully embracing it is the spark for revival.

Authentic Fellowship of Believers

Fellowship in the Early Church was the bedrock of its spiritual vitality and communal strength. Rooted in deep devotion to Christ and one another, believers lived out a shared life, demonstrating their unity in heart and mind. The Scripture affirms, "They devoted themselves to the apostles' teaching and fellowship, to the breaking of bread and prayer." That wasn't just casual association but a radical commitment to live together, sharing everything from their possessions to their burdens, embodying a divine community mirroring heaven's values (see Acts 4:32-35). The power of fellowship allowed the Church to thrive, as members constantly encouraged one another, stirred up faith, and witnessed miracles —testaments to God's active presence among them.

This deep sense of fellowship empowered the Early Church to sustain the revival they were experiencing. Persecution, hardship, and poverty could have easily crushed their resolve, but the unbreakable bond they shared made them resilient. Their love and unity became a living testimony, drawing people into the faith. In John 13:35, Jesus told His disciples, "By this everyone will know that you are my disciples, if you love one another." This love was a revival spark, spreading like wildfire and attracting the attention of those longing for an authentic community (see Acts 41-47). By leaning on each other, they built an unstoppable movement that transformed lives and cities.

Revivalist Charles Finney once said, "Revival is nothing more than a new beginning of obedience to God." This new obedience was fueled by fellowship in the Early Church. They were account-able to one another, helping each other live out their faith in purity and power. Through the constant sharing of testimonies, encouragement, and the Word of God, they fanned the flames of revival. Their fellowship was social, spiritual, and catalytic, the secret to sustaining the revival and spreading the gospel across the Roman Empire. The Early Church was not simply a group of believers—they were a living organism, unified and empowered to carry the message of Christ to the world.

The Breaking of Bread: Communion and Generosity Of Meal Sharing

The breaking of bread through communion and shared meals was an essential part of the Early Church's practice: "So continu-ing daily with one accord in the temple, and breaking bread from house to house, they ate their food with gladness and simplicity of heart" (Acts 32:46). It was the kind of spiritual glue that binds believers together:

Smith Wigglesworth (1859–1947) said, As we partake of the Lord's Table, we proclaim His death and resurrection and feed on His life. The very act of communion lifts us into the spiritual realm, where we commune with Him and receive the power to live in His victory. To Wigglesworth, communion was a source of spiritual power and victory that was critical to sustaining revival in the lives of believers. This practice of communion and meal-sharing strengthened the Early Church's unity and identification with each other and the Lord.

Expressing the importance of the Lord's Supper to the Church, **Dwight L. Moody** eloquently stated, "The table of the Lord is a table of unity. It is a place where we lay aside our differences and come together as one Body to remember Christ's sacrifice and share in the blessings of His grace." We eat the bread and drink the cup, to proclaim the Lord's death till He comes"

(1 Corinthians 11:26) - The price Christ paid on the Cross to purchase our freedom from sin and the message for us to carry to the ends of the earth.

Meal sharing reinforces the unity of the Body and the heart of generosity towards each other. It strengthens the bonds of unity, fellowship, and generosity among the saints, attracting others into the fold (see Acts 4:32-35) ass the revival fire stayed ablaze.

Many churches have picnics and other food events that bring them together. However, it must be more than an eating frenzy common in many church circles today. Meal sharing must center around the fellowship of brotherly love that transcends cultural, racial, denominational, and political barriers – reinforcing authentic fellowship. We must be cautious, however, not to over-emphasize meal sharing as if it is the primary medium of bringing the congregation together but Christ through the teaching of the Word and prayer.

The Power of Prayer

Prayer is the engine of every revival. As **Andrew Murray** said, "If we are to see revival, we must begin with the Church; and if we begin with the Church, we must begin with prayer."

The Early Church was a praying Church, constantly seeking God's will and guidance. Every great revival has been born out of and sustained by earnest prayer. Prayer is, therefore, the lifeblood of any significant movement of God. Under severe threats from the Jewish religious leaders, the early believers and the apostles prayed to the Lord to stay the course and sustain the revival fire.

Acts chapter 4, thus, records their prayer and how the Lord responded to sustain the revival: "Now, Lord, look on their threats and grant to Your servants that with all boldness they may speak Your word, by stretching out Your hand to heal, and that signs and wonders may be done through the name of Your holy Servant Jesus." And when they had prayed, the place where they were assembled was shaken; and all of them were filled with the Holy Spirit, and they spoke the word of God with boldness" (Acts 4:29-31).

Prayer unites the Church with purposes and empowers God's people to stand firm against spiritual opposition. That was true with the Early Church and remained so with all revival movements throughout the history of the Church. They prioritized prayer in their individual and corporate life and worship to keep the revival fire continually burning (see Acts 2:44- 45, Acts 4:23-31, and Acts 12:5). It is through prayer that revival is birthed and sustained.

Unbreakable Unity

The Early Church also recognized the valuable nature of unity in keeping the revival fire burning. As **John Calvin** said, "There is no greater evidence of the reality of Christianity than the unity of believers." The Church United is a powerful, unpenetrable, and unstoppable force to reckon with.

Jesus prayed for our unity: "I do not pray for these alone, but also for those who [1]will believe in Me through their word; that they all may be one, as You, Father, *are* in Me, and I in You; that they also may be one in Us, that the world may believe that You sent Me. And the glory which You gave Me I have given them, that they may be one just as We are one: I in them, and You in Me; that they may be made perfect in one, and that the world may know that You have sent Me, and have loved them as You have loved Me" (John 17:20-23).

The Lord knew that a divided Church would be unable to withstand the enemy's relentless onslaughts. Therefore, we must put aside our sectarian differences and diligently work towards rebuilding the hedges of unity to keep the revival fire burning bright.

The great Puritan preacher **Richard Baxter** summed up true unity: "Unity in essentials, liberty in non-essentials, and clarity in all things." Through oneness or unity of purpose, the Church gives a powerful witness to our fractured world and keeps the revival fire burning.

Our unity is not by uniformity but by divine truth and purpose. A divided body is easy prey in the enemy's grips. The Psalmist asked, "Why have You broken down its walls *and* hedges So that all who pass by pick its fruit?" (Psalm 80:12 AMP). Disunity in the Church erects a signpost inviting the intruders: ***DEMONS WELCOME; THERE IS NO RESISTANCE, AND NO PASSWORD NEEDED.*** Let us rebuild the hedges of unity and keep the flames of revival burning brighter.

The Path Forward: A Revival That Lasts

Revival isn't a one-time event—it's a movement that must be nurtured and sustained through prayer, fellowship, the Word of God, and unity. Let us embrace the Scriptural strategy of impactful and sustained revival, "And they continued steadfastly in apostles' doctrine, fellowship, breaking bread, and prayer" (Acts 2:24). Tha*t* was the Early Church's strategy that allowed them to stay the course and kept the flames of the revival of those days burning despite persecution. The approach is as effective and powerful today as it was then. Any deviation from the plan laid down by the Holy Spirit could trap us in a revival-quenching snare.

INTERNAL FACTORE THAT QUENCH REVIVAL - PART I

Do not quench [subdue, or be unresponsive to the working and guidance of] the [Holy] Spirit. Do not scorn or reject gifts of prophecy or prophecies [spoken revelations—words of instruction, exhortation, or warning]. But test everything carefully [to recognize what is good]. Hold firmly to that which is good **– 1 Thessalonians 5:19-21 AMP.**

The Lord desires to move mightily among His covenant people – the Church. Since the Day of Pentecost, the Church has experienced manifestations of the Glory of the Lord in many dimensions through the power of the Holy Spirit in their worship.

However, the Church faced attacks from the Jewish religious leaders who deemed Christ, His teachings, and followers heretical and a threat to their religious control (see Acts 4:18). The political establishment – The Roman Rule considered the Church an opposition to its power.

A historical example was when, in 64 AD, a devastating fire broke out, ravaging much of Rome (the city). Many believed Emperor Nero himself was responsible, yet he made the Church a convenient scapegoat, accusing the believers of starting the fire.

Nero's accusation led to an intense persecution of the early Christians. Many were arrested, tortured, and executed in horrific ways, including being burned alive, crucified, and torn apart by wild animals in public spectacles. Sadly, persecution and other attempts to silence the Church and quench the fire of revival continue even to this day.

Besides these outside attacks and efforts to quench revival fire, there are factors and elements from within the Church that war against the moving of the Spirit. That has been the experience of past revivals, including the Wesleyan, Welsh, and Azusa revivals.

Let us take a look into the corridors of Church History and consider the external and internal attempts made to quench the Wesleyan Revival:

The Wesleyan Example

The external or outside pressure from the political establishment was relentless against the Wesleyan revival. The revival took place in England at a time of great social and political upheaval. The ruling class was wary of any movement that could potentially upset the social order and viewed the revival with suspicion. The authorities often cracked down on revival meetings. They considered any preaching against social ills dangerous to public order.

The revival also encountered fierce opposition (internal forces) from the Church of England (Anglican or the Episcopal Church). As the state Church and the dominant religious institution in England, the Anglican leaders and clergy members were hostile toward the revivals, considering it a threat to their ecclesiastical authority.

King Solomon wisely stated, "What has been will be again, what has been done will be done again; there is nothing new under the sun" (Ecclesiastes 1:o NIV). Persecution of the Church has been a recurring phenomenon since its inception. Some of the same external and internal revival-quenching forces are still with us. They continue to impede the move of the Holy Spirit within the Church.

In the last two chapters, the rest of the book will explore some potential internal revival-quenching factors to understand how they infiltrate the Church to work against the moving of the Spirit among God's people. Some of the factors may appear harmless or beneficial in the eyes of humanity, but they are contrary to God's plan and purposes for a revival fire to glow.

Working or Cooperating With God

Every outbreak of revival is solely God's doing and not human's. As per the title of this book, ***Anticipating Revival: Positioning the Church for Fresh Fire***, the role of the Church and its leadership is to position the people of God to anticipate, welcome, and embrace the visitation of the Holy Spirit as we cooperate with Him. Cooperating with God is not passive but an active surrender and a willingness to partner with Him in what He is doing. That has been the pattern since the Church began. God is not seeking servants to work for Him but sons and daughters to partner with Him.

Andrew Murray, missionary and intercessor, noted, "We are not called to be workers in God's vineyard, but to be branches connected to the true vine. Our role is to abide in Christ and allow His life to flow through us, bearing fruit for His glory."

It is not about what we can do for God but what God can do through us as we yield to His leading. That is God's mode of operation, especially during seasons of revival. That was the case with the Welsh, Azusa, Lewis Islands, and the Toronto Revivals.

They cooperated with the Lord, and the heavens opened upon them with an outpouring of Fresh Fire.

However, as a revival fire spreads, human tendencies creep in as some leaders begin to think they must work to help the Holy Spirit instead of waiting in faith with expectancy and cooperating with Him as recipients of the wind of the blessings.

Revival historians have, thus, said why the Welsh Revival and countless others ended, ***"God works, and the devil goes to work to resist. God then works all the more. Man goes to work, and the revival comes to an end."***

The works mentality of humanity does not enhance revival nor produce the righteousness of God. **Oswald Chambers** cautioned, "A works mentality can lead to self-righteousness and a reliance on human effort, rather than relying on the power and transforming work of the Holy Spirit. True revival requires a humble dependence on God's grace and surrender to His will."

God is God all by Himself and can do without us, but we are nothing without Him. Whatever God starts, He finishes Himself. The Almighty God does not need any person, man or woman, to complete what He starts. God is all-sufficient and capable. The Scripture affirms, "He who has begun a good work in you will [continue to] perfect *and* complete it until the day of Christ Jesus [the time of His return]" (Philippians 1:6 AMP).

Let us keep in mind that God is not looking to us to do His work. He, instead, invites us to partner or cooperate with what He is doing. As we cooperate, God works with us, through us, and in us to accomplish His purposes to our benefit. That is how we can keep the revival fire burning. Doing otherwise could quench or impede the move of God.

Resistance From The Previous Wave

Resistance from previous spiritual waves has often stifled new moves of God, as traditions and sectarian prejudices shape how many believers expect revival to unfold. The Sovereign Lord, however, is not bound by human expectations; He pours out His Spirit in diverse ways, choosing the instruments and channels through which His blessings flow. Though the Holy Spirit is the same in every revival, His manifestations and dimensions can differ. This variability challenges believers to trust in God's sovereignty rather than insist on revival happening in ways they are familiar with or taught in their denominational settings.

Unfortunately, history shows that many who fervently pray for revival are often the same ones who resist it when it comes because it does not align with their expectations. Leaders in the Church, especially, must resist the temptation to criticize new spiritual movements that feel unfamiliar or uncomfortable. Instead of dismissing what seems different, they should encourage discernment, openness to God's leading, and a humble willingness to align with the Spirit's work, no matter how unconventional it may appear. That is crucial for ensuring congregations are not deprived of experiencing God's blessings.

History shows that some leaders lashed vehement criticisms of the Welsh Revival of 1904-1905, which brought thousands of people to faith in Christ and sparked a wave of worldwide missionary activity. Feeling threatened by the revival, some church leaders rejected the idea of a new spiritual awakening. The revival's leader, Evan Roberts, was ridiculed as being too emotional and lacking theological training. Some ministers and leaders even discouraged their congregations from attending the meetings.

Critics, typically driven by rigid ideas of how the Spirit should manifest, hinder others from participating in and receiving the revival's benefits. The same pattern repeats, where leaders, like the Pharisees of Jesus' time, prevented themselves and their followers from entering the flow of God's work.

The Lord strongly condemns such behavior, "But woe (judgment is coming) to you, [self-righteous] scribes and Pharisees, hypocrites, because you shut off the kingdom of heaven in front of people; for you do not enter yourselves, nor do you allow those who are [in the process of] entering to do so" (Matthew 23:13 AMP).

This resistance, fueled by spiritual pride and preconceived notions, leads to missed opportunities for experiencing a fresh move of the Spirit.

Believers today must heed the warnings of **A. B. Simpson**, a participant of both the Welsh and the Azusa revivals urging openness to God's unexpected ways: "Let us not be so wedded to our own opinions and traditions that we cannot recognize the hand of God when it is moving in a new and unexpected way. The Spirit is always at work; let us be open and receptive to His leading. We must not allow our traditions or insecurities to stifle the Spirit's work. Instead of resisting, we should surrender to the Spirit's leading because no human effort can withstand the power of God's sovereign plans (see Job 42:2). By humbly aligning ourselves with the Spirit, we can avoid impeding the flow of revival and fully partake in the blessings God desires to pour out on His people.

Unbelief

Revival comes upon those who hold fast to the Word and diligently seek the Lord with unwavering faith through prayer. Unbelief is the climatic element that causes spiritual drought. Doubt and unbelief are the enemies of the faith and the thieves of the blessings of revival. They cripple the Church and hinder the manifestation of God's power among His people. Revival comes when the people of God embrace faith and, with desperation, invest in earnest prayer.

In the Old Testament, the Israelites repeatedly doubted God's ability to deliver them and lost faith in His promises, resulting in periods of spiritual dryness and apostasy. Similarly, in the

New Testament, Jesus could not do many miracles in his hometown of Nazareth because of the people's unbelief.

James warns, "... he that wavers are like a wave of the sea driven with the wind and tossed. For let not that man think that he shall receive anything of the Lord. A double-minded man *is* unstable in all his ways" (James 1:6-8).

The power of God was not diminished in Jesus at His hometown. The Scripture declares, "And He did not do many miracles there [in Nazareth] because of their unbelief" (Matthew 13:58 AMP). It wasn't the devil that stopped miracles from happening—though he plays a role in spiritual battles—but the lack of faith among the people. As believers, we must resist the temptation to always point to the devil as the cause of spiritual drought. Instead, we must look hard at our hearts and conduct - a self-inventory of our faith. Unbelief can be a far more significant hindrance to the move of God than we may realize.

Revivalists like Charles Finney, Jonathan Edwards, D.L. Moody, and Evan Roberts understood this truth well. Finney declared that unbelief binds the hands of God's people, preventing them from accessing His strength. Edwards saw unbelief as the dampness that extinguishes the fire of revival. Moody described unbelief as the enemy of revival, stifling faith and quenching the Holy Spirit's work. Similarly, Roberts warned that revival cannot flourish where unbelief is present, urging believers to cultivate a faith that burns like a flame. These insights remind us that doubt directly undermines the move of God.

The Church today must heed these warnings and guard against unbelief as we position ourselves for a fresh outpouring of God's Spirit. True revival and spiritual awakening are impossible in an atmosphere clouded by doubt. As the Body of Christ, we must foster an unwavering belief in God's promises and His ability to work mightily in our midst. Faith is the key to unlocking the miraculous and ushering in revival. God will move powerfully in our midst as we stand in faith, anticipating Fresh Fire.

The leaders of the Wesleyan, Welsh, and Azusa Street revivals waited on the Lord with faith in His promise to pour His Spirit upon all flesh (see Joel 2:28-29). Prayer for revival is never in a vacuum but rooted in faith in the Word of God. Unless we mix our prayer with faith, it is an empty noise.

Divisions Over Non-Essentials

It is not uncommon to see various religious groups claiming doctrinal or theological superiority over others. Within the Christian faith, denominations and church groups differ in beliefs and practices. However, it is disheartening when believers use these differences to assert spiritual superiority and create division within the Body of Christ.

It is even more disheartening and even dangerous when spiritual superiority manifests during a revival in such statements by believers: ***But they do not believe as we do***, or ***They do not worship like us***, or ***They still sing the same old hymns***, or ***Their pastors do not preach like our pastors***, and on and on.

Sadly, some believers try extremely hard to find every reason possible to distinguish their denomination or little groupings from others with a sense of spiritual pride. There is nothing wrong with holding to our convictions. However, a conviction not undergirded by love makes the possessor of that conviction obnoxious and the dogma possessor impulsive. We must learn to reason with one another through a Christ-like attitude over our differences.

At this point, I must again quote the statement of the 17th-century Puritan preacher Richard Baxter, "Unity in essentials, liberty in non-essentials, and clarity in all things." Jesus Christ is **"the essential,"** but all others are **"the non-essentials."**

As followers of Christ, we are to love one another and work toward unity based on what we have in common – Jesus Christ and Him crucified. Jesus Himself prayed for this unity among believers in John 17:21, saying, "That they may all be one, just as you, Father, are in me, and I in you, that they also may be in us, so that the world may believe that you have sent me."

The unity the Scripture calls for does not imply we must all be in the same denomination or church groupings, have the same traditions, or sing the same kind of songs. It is not a call to lose one's identity like merging denominations or changing local church names. Instead, we must reinforce our true oneness and identity in Christ as a blood-bought part and parcel of His body That is "**the essential**." However, when we focus on these non-essential differences, we risk losing sight of what truly matters – Jesus Christ.

As a starting point to see a revival, we must seek the Lord in humility rather than dwelling on our differences. We must re-member that the Body of Christ comprises many members with unique gifts and contributions (see 1 Corinthians 12:12- 27). Yet all are called to work towards unity and love each other as Christ has loved us (see John 13:34-35).

We cannot tackle all the revival-quenching elements in this volume. However, we shall touch on a few more in the next chapter.

INTERNAL FACTOR THAT QUENCH REVIVAL - PART II

And do not grieve the Holy Spirit of God, by whom you were sealed for the day of redemption **– Ephesians 4:30.**

In our materialistic and pleasure-mad age, acquiring wealth is the day's order. Its slogan, " What you see is what you get, " has made it much easier for humanity to excuse the eternal (spiritual) for the temporal (carnal), ignoring the spiritual for what we can see, hear, smell, taste, and touch. Such canal-mindedness has even found its way into the pulpits and pews of the Church, quenching the longing of many for Fresh Fire.

Therefore, it is no surprise that Apostle Paul cautioned the Church not to quench nor grieve the Spirit: "And do not grieve the Holy Spirit of God by whom you were sealed for the day of redemption" (Ephesians 4:30). We must undertake self-evaluation to identify and repent of attitudes and behaviors in our lives that are not pleasing to the Lord. Those can grieve the Holy Spirit and hinder the move of God among His people - the Church.

Many early revivalists recognized and addressed a critical issue: the detrimental effects of pride and self-sufficiency on spiritual revival. They warned that when we rely on our own abilities and refuse to humble ourselves before God, we stifle the outpouring of His presence.

Our human carnal tendencies include trying to operate independently of the Holy Spirit, resisting Him by ignoring the Word and falling into spiritual pride, trying to outsmart the Holy Spirit, and even attempting to control and manage His manifestation among God's people. We must, instead, yield to His leadership. Let us dive a little deeper into some of these revival-quenching elements.

Attempts To Manage The Holy Spirit

As masterfully stated by Rev. Billy Graham, "You cannot confine the Holy Spirit to a program or a set of rules. He moves as He pleases, and we must be willing to follow."

If we believe God is sovereign, all-powerful, and all-knowing, we will follow His leading and not interfere with His actions. Any attempt to control, manage, or manipulate the move of God is an indication of unbelief, especially when we assume we can handle things better without Him.

During a revival, everyone appears to enjoy and move with the unorthodox and spontaneous flow of worship and manifestations of the Spirit. However, in their vain attempt to exert control over the revival, some leaders try to manage, regulate, and systematize the operation and manifestations of the Spirit.

Out of ignorance and misplaced humility, others follow the Rebekah Syndrome: *I know and believe God is capable, but I must help Him* (see Genesis 24:21-23 and 27:1-33). That does not enhance revival but hinders the flow of the Spirit in the Church.

Let us humbly remember that *God is God without us, but we are nothing without Him. He does not need our vote or approval to be God.*

Revival is all God's doing and not us. The pastor, author, and theologian, **A. W. Tozer**, made this striking observation about the role of the Holy Spirit in the Church, "If the Holy Spirit were withdrawn from the Church today, 95 percent of what we do would go on, and no one would know the difference. If the Holy Spirit had been withdrawn from the New Testament Church, 95 percent of what they did would stop, and everybody would know the difference."

We shall see marvelous manifestations of the Spirit when we step out of His way and let Him do as He pleases. The Holy Spirit does not need a teacher or a manager. He is sovereign. The Prophet Isaiah poses this question to the Church, "Who has directed the Spirit of the Lord, Or has taught Him as His counselor? Who taught Him the path of justice and knowledge, and informed Him of the way of understanding?" (Isaiah 40:13-14 AMP). The answer is obvious: *NO ONE*. The Holy Spirit is omniscient, complete, and capable, needing no human advice or instruction. He is self-existent.

Spiritual Arrogance Of Exclusivity

Exclusivity, rooted in self-centeredness, is a despicable display of spiritual pride and arrogance. It is pervasive in *cultish* church environments. Those within such circles keep to themselves, considering all others spiritually unacceptable.

Folks within such circles are often preoccupied with religious traditions and rituals. They rely on outward forms and ceremonies without a genuine heart transformation. That is a hindrance to the manifestation of revival.

The Pharisees of Jesus' days were known for such spiritual arrogance of exclusivity, as evident in the following exchange:

"And when the scribes and Pharisees saw Jesus eating with the tax collectors and sinners, they said to His disciples, "How *is it* that He eats and drinks with tax collectors and sinners?" (Mark 2:16).

The Lord responded to their inquiries with a stern rebuke of their exclusivity, "Those who are well do not need a physician, but those who are sick. But go and learn what *this* means: 'I desire mercy and not sacrifice. For I did not come to call the righteous, but sinners, to repentance" (Matthew 9:10-13).

The spiritual pride of arrogant exclusivity implies that their adherents only reach out to those who act, think, and look like them. Church groups with this attitude see themselves as having the perfect theology and judge all other church groups and ministries by their denominational traditions and not by the Word of God.

We must follow Jesus's example to reach all people regardless of denominational, doctrinal, national, racial, and social background. Revivals occur amidst a diverse population of denominational, social, ethnic, and political persuasions. No particular denomination, church grouping, nationality, or race has an exclusive right over whom and how the Holy Spirit torches with Fresh Fire. Revival units and not divide the people of God.

The starting point to break the strongholds of arrogant exclusivity is focusing on Jesus Christ. May our supper-imposed theology of spiritual pride, prejudices, and arrogance dissolve in the fire of the Spirit. The Wesleyan, Welsh, and Azusa Revivals did not occur on denominational preferences and *spiritual* exclusivity but on the message of Salvation by Grace through the power of the Holy Spirit.

Turning Emotional Experiences Into Doctrines

Being in a revival environment is impossible without experiencing excitement and an overflow of emotions. With daily occurrences of signs and wonders during the revivals of the Early Church, the believers had an explosion of emotional experiences. However, the revival fire stayed ablaze not because of the emotional excitement but because "... they continued steadfastly in the apostles' doctrine (the teachings of Jesus), in fellowship, in the breaking of bread, and prayer" (Acts 2:42).

Emotions are a part of the human experience and are not necessarily dangerous or harmful. However, as we anticipate revival, exercising caution is imperative to avoid the temptation of elevating emotional experiences into a new ecclesiastical rule of thumb above the Word of God. The Word remains the final authority and guide to our spiritual and moral well-being (see 2 Timothy 3:16).

As God's people, we must endeavor through the Holy Spirit to distinguish an authentic worship experience where one encounters the presence of God from sheer emotionalism. **Asahel Nettleton** warned the Church of the danger of confusing emotions with the Holy Spirit's presence, saying, "Many seem to mistake the fervors of animal passion for the operations of the Spirit of God. The genuine work of the Spirit of God is unattainable with such confusion and tumultuous emotion."

The Church's solid theological foundation is on Scripture rather than subjective emotional experiences. Past Christian leaders like Billy Graham and Charles Spurgeon spoke to the Church of the reality of the Word of God as the final authority and the basis of our faith over and above emotional experiences. **Billy warned** we must always be careful not to confuse our emotions with the leading of the Holy Spirit. The Spirit leads us through the Word of God, not through our feelings. **Spurgeon** said It is a grave mistake to suppose that feelings are always to be relied upon in matters of religion.

When emotions become the focus, they can lead to severe challenges as different factions argue over subjective matters –

trying to determine which particular emotional expressions are or are not Biblical. That could fuel unhealthy comparisons, especially when it becomes the standard of measuring spirituality.

Attempts To Outdo Others And Outsmart The Spirit

There is an ongoing battle between the flesh and the spirit within our human nature. That has brewed the ugly tendency of many to want to outshine others and even outsmart the Holy Spirit if that were possible.

Apostle Paul declares, "But I say, walk *habitually* in the [Holy] Spirit [seek Him and be responsive to His guidance], and then you will certainly not carry out the desire of the [sinful nature [which responds impulsively without regard for God and His precepts]. For the sinful nature has its desire which is opposed to the Spirit, and the [desire of the] Spirit opposes the [sinful nature; for these, [two, the sinful nature and the Spirit] are in direct opposition to each other [continually in conflict], so that you [as believers] do not [always] do whatever [good things] you want to do" (Galatians 5:16-18 AMP).

That battle continues to rage. During the revival of the Early Church, a couple, Ananias and his wife, Sapphira, attempted to outshine the others and outsmart the Holy Spirit. They sold their land to give the proceeds to the Church but kept back part of the proceeds and lied about it to the apostles.

Their actions incurred a swift divine judgment as Peter had this to say to Ananias, "Ananias, why has Satan filled your heart to lie to the Holy Spirit and kept back part of the price of the land for yourself? .... You have not lied to man but God" (Acts 5:3-4). And to Sapphira, his wife and collaborator, Peter said, "How is it that you have agreed together to test the Holy Spirit of the Lord?" (Acts 5:9). The couple immediately died following Peter's statement.

Also, during the revival in Samaria, Peter had some stern words for Simon, a sorcerer who thought he could give the apostle money for the power to lay hands on others to receive the baptism of the Holy Spirit, "You have neither part nor portion in this matter, for your heart is not right in the sight of God. Therefore, repent your wickedness, and pray to God if the thought of your heart may be forgiven. For I see you are poisoned by bitterness and iniquity" (Acts 8:21-23).

In both examples above, we see how people, amid a mighty move of God, allowed their fleshly nature to overrule their spirit to attempt consciously or subconsciously to outsmart the Holy Spirit. That is a revival quenches recipe.

A word of caution: "Attempting to outsmart the Spirit of the Living God is dangerous to the Church's spiritual health." In many instances, the attempt to outsmart the Holy Spirit manifests in cover-ups of failures, either moral (sexual and financial) or spiritual(deviation from the truth and spiritual manipulations of the people of God) by those in leadership. Many great ministries and leaders have seen their abrupt ends or plummeted into disgrace because they had tried to outsmart God.

At all costs, let us step aside and let God be God over His Church. We must, individually and corporately, repent of any of the above attitudes lurking in our hearts. They quench revival and stand in the way of positioning the Church for Fresh Fire.

In His loving kindness, the Lord has given us examples of these revival-quenching attitudes in His Word to guide our behavior and attitudes during seasons of revival. It is, therefore, our responsibility, with the help of the Holy Spirit, to uproot and dispose of them from our lives.

Beloved, let us get all the revival-quenching garbage out of the way for the Holy Spirit to keep the fire of revival burning in our lives, churches, ministries, and communities.

TRIBUTE TO MY MOTHER

With much humility, boundless admiration, and an enduring wellspring of love and affection, I bestow this book as a tribute to the most cherished soul of my existence, my dearest mother, Dora.

Over eight decades ago, you were baptized in the Holy Spirit, and from that moment, your life has been a testament to faith, love, worship, and profound wisdom. Your oft-repeated words, "I am helpless without the anointing of the Holy Spirit," resonate as a guiding virtue for all fortunate to witness your remarkable journey.

As an intercessor and active participant in one of the most significant outpourings of the Holy Spirit in Ghana, you have witnessed miracles, watching the dead brought back to life and the afflicted miraculously healed from a myriad of ailments. Your unwavering devotion to Christ and your indomitable character, marked by courage, loyalty, spiritual fortitude, boundless com-passion, and unparalleled generosity, have served as a lighthouse for all of us.

Your existence embodies the essence of the Virtuous Woman, as described in Proverbs 31:10, and your life of zeal and unwaver-ing commitment paints a portrait of grace and strength for all to behold. Indeed, you were the radiant crown that adorned the head of my beloved father, J. B. Amankwatia, just as Proverbs 12:4 extols.

This tribute is but a humble offering, an admiration of a life illuminated by faith, a life that has kindled the spirits of countless souls, and a life that continues to shine as a beacon of love, resilience, and courage.

In dedicating this book to you, Mom, I honor your name and the extraordinary legacy of faith and love you have sculpted into our hearts. You are, and forever will be, the human guiding star of our lives.

Your beautiful life of impactful, spirit-filled existence is like a sweet fragrance that reaches beyond your immediate surroundings to all who know you.

REFLECTIONS ON DORA'S LIFE BY HER MOST AMAZING GRANDSONS

"Nana, you are one of the most anointed and blessed souls to walk this earth. Your influence has touched countless lives, all through the grace and goodness of God. The legacy you've built, rooted in love, faith, and unwavering strength, will be forever cherished by the family and friends who honor you. Your life has been a beacon of inspiration, and for that, Grandma, I stand in awe and salute you."

— *Daniel Opoku Amankwatia*

"Grandma, you are an extraordinary and priceless gift—a woman filled with the Holy Spirit whose every action reflects the love and grace of God. Your warmth, kindness, and tenderness have nurtured generations, shaping us with your wisdom and love. As a mother, grandmother, and great-grandmother, your words have lifted hearts, your praise has inspired greatness, and your virtuous life continues to shine as a guiding light for us all. You are the embodiment of godly wisdom, and we are forever blessed to have you."

— *Asamoah Gyawu Amankwatia*

"Nana, you are the heart of my world because your love is genuine, and your care for me is boundless. You are anointed with wisdom, and your sharp mind, discerning spirit, and vibrant sense of humor are unmatched. The way you impart life's lessons with such clarity and grace is a rare gift, and your presence is irreplaceable. You are, without question, the best."
— *Scott Bobie Amankwatia*